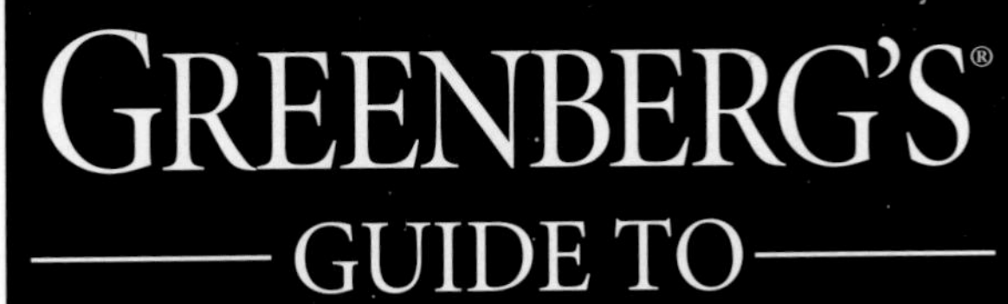

AURORA® SLOT CARS

Thomas Graham

© 1995 Thomas Graham. All rights reserved. This book may not be reproduced in whole or in part, by any means, without written permission from the publisher, except in the case of brief quotations used in reviews. Published by Greenberg Books, a division of Kalmbach Publishing Co., 21027 Crossroads Circle, Waukesha, Wisconsin 53187. Phone: (414) 796-8776.

Printed in the United States of America

97 98 99 00 01 02 03 04 05 06 10 9 8 7 6 5 4 3 2

Publisher's Cataloging-in-Publication Data
(Prepared by Quality Books, Inc.)

Graham, Thomas, 1943–.
Greenberg's guide to Aurora slot cars /
Tom Graham. —Waukesha, WI : Greenberg
Pub., 1995.
p. cm.
Includes index.
ISBN 0-89778-400-6

1. Automobiles—models. 2. Model car
racing. I. Title. II. Title: Guide to Aurora
Slot cars.

TF237.G73 1995 629.22'1
QBI95-20355

Book design: Kristi Ludwig

Aurora® is a registered trademark of Tomy America. This book is neither authorized nor approved by Tomy America.

Contents

Acknowledgments

AMONG THE GREATEST pleasures derived from researching this book was meeting the people who love little electric cars—people who, like me, celebrate the romance of the slotted road. Many of these individuals know far more about this subject than I, and I freely acknowledge my debt to them. Among the most helpful sources of information were Greg Holland, Jim Johnson, Dave Lockwood, Ron Esterline, Phil Frank, Mark Mattei, Scott Ronhock, Edward Sourbeck, Kevin Timothy, and Bill Wessels. Howard Kilgore read the manuscript.

Photographs of HO and 1/48 scale cars were taken in the home of Bob Beers, to whom I give enormous thanks. Dave Lockwood furnished his AFX cars for the photo shoot. Photos of the 1/32, 1/25, and 1/24 cars were taken by Gary Gerding. Among the cars in these photos are some loaned by Bernard Sampson and Emil Bertolini.

Detailed information on colors, model variations, and prices came from Bob Beers and Howard Johansen. Every serious slot car collector needs to subscribe to Bob's *HO C.A.R.S.* and purchase the latest edition of Howard's *Slot Car Value Guide.*

The perspective from inside the Aurora plant was supplied by many individuals intimately connected with the company. I would first like to thank Marie Cuomo, Maria Shikes, Eleanor Giammarino, and Joseph Giammarino, who together with John Cuomo and Abe Shikes first agreed to the formation of Aurora over dinner in Brooklyn in 1950. Thanks also to Mr. Charles M. Diker, Aurora president in the 1970s.

The list of other former Aurora personnel and hobby industry leaders who helped me encompasses an awesome array of talent and experience: Robert Bernhard, Derek Brand, John E. Brodbeck, Frank Carver, Richard Cohen, Raymond Haines, Kenneth Hill, Homer Hleovas, Jim Keeler, Jim Kirby, Michael Meyers, Walter Moe, Richard Palmer, Nat Polk, Richard Ratkiewich, Jim Russell, Richard Schwarzchild, Donald "Bill" Silverstein, and John Vernon.

Chris Becker, Kalmbach Publishing Co. photographer, shot the car photos at Bob Beers' home; Jim Bunte directed the shoot and skillfully edited my manuscript. Mary Algozin proofed the book at Greenberg in Milwaukee.

Thanks is also due the staff of the periodicals section of the Library of Congress, and to Maurice and David Gherman, who gave me access to the archives of *Craft, Model and Hobby Industry Magazine.*

My deepest thanks to all of the above—and to many others too numerous to mention—who shared their knowledge with me and often saved me from errors of fact and interpretation. Any mistakes that may have escaped their notice are my responsibility.

Preface

AURORA IS THE NAME from which toy legends have arisen. For nearly 30 years, Aurora Plastics Corporation led the way in popularizing some of the most spectacularly successful hobbies of the modern era, including plastic model kits and electric slot cars. Because Aurora created innovative and intriguing products, produced them well, and showed enterprise in marketing them, it rose by the 1960s to become the world's largest hobby company. In the 1970s Aurora expanded even further, becoming one of the nation's foremost producers of tabletop games. Then, in the tumultuous business climate of the 1970s, Aurora disappeared. The untimely demise only adds to their mystique.

Today Aurora's classic plastic model kits and slot cars are highly collectible. My goal in writing this book is to provide accurate information to collectors about Aurora slot cars manufactured between 1960 and 1977, the year of Aurora's demise. I'll also explain the origins of slot cars, give an inside-the-factory look at how Aurora made its cars, and relate the story of how slot car racing became one of the most popular pastimes of the 1960s and 1970s.

1

SLOT CARS
a fast start

Aurora's founders: John Cuomo, Abe Shikes, and Joe Giammarino. Photo courtesy *Rod & Custom Models.*

Like all toymaking legends, Aurora comes from the most humble of origins. Aurora Plastics Corporation received its charter from the state of New York on March 9, 1950, beginning operations in August from a converted Brooklyn garage on 62nd Street. The early days saw Aurora as a contract molding shop, making plastic products for a variety of customers, mostly in the novelty jewelry business. Soon it was plastic clothes hangers and toy bow and arrow sets for dime stores—very basic jobs for a small molding company.

Then in the fall of 1952, Aurora made a decided change of direction and introduced its inexpensive all-plastic model airplane kits. Not only were the kits among the first of their kind, but Aurora's products were marketed through chain stores—an industry first.

With a single product launch, Aurora brought modeling out of sidestreet hobby shops and into Main Street variety stores. In large part because of these inexpensive Aurora kits, model building became the most popular hobby of 1950s American boys.

The founding

Abe Shikes. Joseph Giammarino. In no uncertain terms, they were two redefiners of postwar toy marketing and manufacturing.

Shikes was born in Russia in 1908 and moved to New York City in the 1920s, where he made his career manufacturing inexpensive jewelry. Short in stature, emotional, and aggressive by nature, Shikes brought tough-minded leadership to Aurora. Brooklyn native Giammarino was a perfect complement to Shikes. Joe was from a family of jewelry makers—and also happened to be a college-trained electrical engineer. At Aurora, Shikes did the talking and Giammarino made the machinery run.

The pair founded Aurora with the financial backing of silent partners. The 1952 departure of those partners forced a reorganization of the company. Enter John Cuomo, the third major figure in Aurora's rise. Born in Italy in 1901, Cuomo came aboard as sales manager and junior partner. Personable and outgoing, Cuomo was Aurora's spokesman to advertisers, distributors, and retailers.

Brisk demand for Aurora plastic models caused the young company to quickly outgrow its makeshift Brooklyn facility. Aurora moved to a large, modern plant in December 1953. The location—44 Cherry Valley Road, West Hempstead, Long Island—would remain Aurora headquarters throughout the rest of the firm's history. Soon after relocation, Aurora initiated production of a hobbycraft line: Coppersmith kits for producing embossed copper plaques; Air Champ Radio, crystal radio kits;

John E. Brodbeck

and by 1959, ready-to-fly model airplanes for department stores.

Model airplanes did well for Aurora. To assure a continuous supply of engines, Aurora in 1960 purchased K&B Allyn, a California manufacturer of gas-powered airplane motors. K&B had been founded in 1944 by Ludwig Kading and John E. Brodbeck. When Aurora bought K&B in 1960, Brodbeck was its manager, an expert designer of model airplane motors and one of the best-known men in the American hobby industry. Aurora moved K&B from Compton to Downey and sent Sheldon "Shellie" Ostrowe from West Hempstead to California to oversee operations, but Brodbeck remained in charge of production.

In 1960 Aurora introduced another hobby product—electric-powered slot cars—and a generation of American youngsters went crazy over them. Aurora and subsidiary K&B emerged as the dominant builders of top-quality slot cars in both the mass-market toy field and the more demanding hobbyist segment.

Perhaps most important, Aurora succeeded in slot cars where others failed because they spent time, energy, and money showing youngsters how to have fun with miniature racers. Slot cars catapulted Aurora to the top of the hobby world—far ahead of model kit rival Revell, and very far ahead of venerable toy manufacturers like Lionel. It was the product line that ultimately defined the West Hempstead manufacturer.

Origins of the slot car

The distant ancestors of Aurora's slot cars were 19th-century windup toy games with racing horses, bicycles, and eventually automobiles. Mechanized toys were among the most popular Industrial Revolution-era playthings; their lifelike animation made them a hit with affluent toy consumers and, later, those of the working class.

Ironically, the closest toy to Aurora's slot cars originated in electric trains—the segment that would ultimately suffer the most with the advent of slot cars. In 1912, the Lionel Corporation, already famous for its electric trains, introduced an electric car set featuring metal 1/24 scale Stutz Bearcats rolling around a steel roadway on rubber tires. Power was transmitted to the car motors by two rails recessed in a slot.

Lionel's cars were sold only through 1916 and today are regarded as scarce collectibles. Though not very successful at retail, the Lionel toys did have one lasting effect: they introduced the concept of toy electric cars to the public. The idea was so basic and solid that it continued to arise again and again, both in Europe and the United States. In 1929 a Kokomo, Indiana, firm marketed an electric car whose front bumper picked up voltage from an electrified fence running alongside the roadway. In 1935 Louis Marx marketed a windup set with cars that operated on a figure-eight roadway. The following year Marx electrified the set. The concept of electric road racing endured, but still didn't capture the toy buying public's attention like electric trains.

Adult hobbyists invented the sport of "rail car" racing in the late 1930s, and it developed a following in Great Britain and the American Midwest during the 1950s. Hobbyists scratchbuilt elaborately detailed wood, fiberglass, and metal cars. The first examples were powered by gasoline engines, tethered to a post, and set to race on a circular track—what became known as thimble-drome racing. Other hobbyists clamped their cars to a fixed, raised rail and turned them loose to run. Soon the rail went electric, and motors were scavenged from model locomotives. For the first time, the speed of an individual car could be controlled by a rheostat.

However, rail racing was a hobby for adults who read *Popular Mechanics*. The skills, tools, and

Lionel 1912 car set
B. Schwab photograph

money needed to build the cars and the tracks were well beyond the average youngster. Noisy, smelly gasoline-powered cars had to stay outdoors, and rail cars—built in a variety of scales, but mostly 1/32—required garage- or basement-sized space for an adequate layout.

British forebears

It was only a matter of time until the toy industry would see the intrinsic entertainment of miniature auto racing and respond with a commercial product. The first company to do so was Scalextric of Britain. The men who introduced Scalextric to America were Irwin and Nathan Polk of New York. Widely regarded as the godfathers of the American hobby industry, the Polks ran an elaborate five-story hobby shop in Manhattan and marketed their own line of products under the Aristo-Craft label. The Polks had been tinkering with the idea of a home race-car set since the 1930s. In 1957 they went to England and made an agreement with Frederick Francis to import his Scalextric home race sets.

Francis introduced Scalextric in England in 1957 and showed sets at the Hobby Industry Association of America (HIAA) show in 1957. The metal 1/30 scale Ferrari and Maserati Formula I race cars rolled on plastic wheels and were touted as capable of scale speeds up to 130 miles per hour. However, to the dismay of the Polks, only two American distributors placed orders, and the next two years in the American toy market were equally barren, saleswise. The reason: a hefty $50 price tag. However, the cars did catch on in Europe. In late 1958 Scalextric was sold to Lines Brothers of England, but the Polks continued as the American distributor for two more years.

While Scalextric was putting large-scale slot cars on the road, real success was still in development—and from a totally independent source.

The father of HO slot cars

Credit for development of the HO slot car must go to Derek

Derek Brand, the father of HO slot cars

Brand. Born in England in 1926, Brand emigrated to the United States in 1948 and went to work for California design company Gowland & Gowland, a toy industry design house that occasionally marketed their own playthings under the Gowland trademark.

Short, balding, and cheery, Brand was a consummate engineer who had long tinkered with the concept of an electric home racing set. In one of his first assignments for Gowland, Brand developed a product that revolutionized the plastic model kit industry—Highway Pioneers plastic car model kits. Brand sculpted patterns from wood, which tooling shops later used to create metal dies central to the newly dominant toymaking medium of injection molding. Creating Highway Pioneers gave Brand the sculpting expertise that would prove so integral to Aurora's later success.

Gowland sold Derek Brand's Highway Pioneers to Revell Inc. of Los Angeles. Revell marketed them as inexpensive hobby items through dime stores. When Aurora's model airplane kits hit the stores shortly after Revell's cars, plastic models were on their way to becoming a cornerstone of the hobby industry.

Jack Gowland relocated his company in 1953 to Puerto Rico to take advantage of tax incentives. Derek Brand also moved and continued his research on an electric car set. Brand's first experiments involved putting Pittman model train motors inside die-cast Dinky cars. Brand supplied the cars with electric current through two strips of metallic paint sprayed onto the roadbed. The results were unsatisfactory: motors were too big and too expensive, and the painted-powerstrip idea just didn't work.

Meanwhile, wanderlust caused Jack Gowland to move to Canada. He turned his company over to Carl Robinette, who proceeded to move everything back to California, settling in Santa Barbara in 1955. One of his spinoff corporations was Crafco, where Brand was reassigned. Derek continued tinkering with his electric car system, agreeing with Robinette to design it in HO scale (1/87), ensuring compatibility with the popular model railroading scale.

Most important, Brand finally solved the problem of supplying miniature racing cars with electricity.

He embedded two metal strips into a plastic road surface. Only one challenge remained—creating the cars.

Birth of the vibrator

With the roadway problem solved, Brand tackled the ongoing dilemma of getting bulky, expensive motors into very small car bodies. His solution was, quite simply, ingenious. Brand designed his own motor using a common door buzzer—the "vibrator" motor. It was small enough to fit in a chassis less than 2" long. Brand got little encouragement from Jack Gowland, who declared, "You'll never make a door buzzer run around a track!" But the defiant Anglo-Californian did just that.

Brand's motor is a model of simplicity. An upright coil of wire becomes an electromagnet when electricity flows through it. The design places a flat metal actuator reed across the top of the coil. When the coil is magnetized by electricity, the actuator reed pulls toward the coil and ratchets a drive gear mounted on the car's rear axle. At the same time, the reed also forces down a rod passing through the coil. The downward motion of the rod pushes the rear end of the electrical pickup shoe away from the bottom of the coil, momentarily breaking electrical contact and demagnetizing the coil.

The actuator reed then springs back up and (at the bottom of the coil) the metal contact shoe does the same thing, reestablishing contact with the coil. This sends current through the coil once again, and the whole process starts anew. With 16 volts of alternating current flowing through the system, the process is repeated many times per second, sending the car literally buzzing down Brand's track.

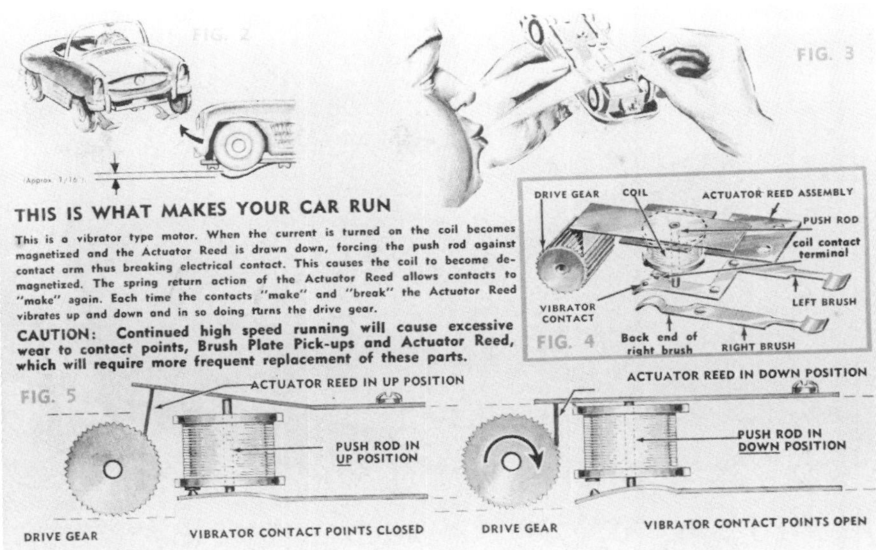

Derek Brand's ingenious vibrator motor design

Highways: the first HO slot car set

Carl Robinette knew he had a winner with Derek Brand's ingenious miniaturized car system. He began shopping the concept around to numerous toy companies, finally cutting a deal with British toymaker Mettoy, builder of Corgi die-cast cars. Mettoy represented a situation similar to that of the Polk brothers—low British tooling and production costs underwriting the launch of a questionable new product. Robinette retained ownership of the tooling, leasing it to Mettoy.

With great fanfare, Mettoy's Playcraft division unveiled Highways Road Transport System at the 1959 Brighton Toy Fair. Unfortunately, most English toy and hobby distributors were unimpressed. Highways arrived on the scene shortly after Scalextric, and it would never achieve the popularity in Great Britain that larger-scale systems would.

During the fair, glum Playcraft marketers received a visit from Abe Shikes and Joe Giammarino of Aurora. Since Playcraft distributed Aurora plastic model kits in Great Britain, Shikes and Giammarino were expected. The two Americans surveyed the miniature car system and were surprised and delighted.

Abe Shikes discovered Derek Brand lurking behind a curtain, like the Wizard of Oz, operating the controls of his slot car layout: "He turned it on and I couldn't believe something so small could have a motor inside. I picked one up and put it down in a hurry—it was hot. Whenever anybody would come in to watch the cars, this Playcraft guy would wet his fingers before picking up a car. He was cooling them off." Playcraft had just 12 handbuilt prototype cars specially built by Brand. Only 4 would go into production: the Jaguar XK140, Mercedes 300SL, Mack Lorry, and to please the anticipated American market, 1958 Chevrolet Impala (nos. 3101 through 3104).

Speed controllers were green-painted metal with working "ignition" keys and tiny steering wheels operating the rheostats. Brand's vibrator motors could endure 150 to 200 hours of operation without breakdown. Previously he'd run numerous home tests, setting up a Highways system on his dining room table and letting cars run while he watched television. Interference on his TV screen reminded Brand that his tiny motors were still humming away.

Although Carl Robinette had taken his slot car concept to Great Britain first, he always intended to market his product in the United States. However, when Abe Shikes and Joe Giammarino asked Robinette for an American license, he refused, saying Aurora wasn't large enough to handle the anticipated high volume.

Playcraft's Highways. Note the exceedingly rare Chevy Impala (3103) at left, as well as the Jaguar XK-140 (3101), Mercecdes 300SL (3102), and Ford Lorry (3104).

Robinette returned to the U.S. after Brighton and tried to sell Highways to a number of big American toy manufacturers (including Mattel and A. C. Gilbert) but found no takers. Only then—and only after much persuasion by Shikes—did Robinette agree to license his car system to Aurora.

Launching HO in the States

Aurora introduced Highways to the American hobby industry in January 1960 at the Hobby Industry Association of America show in Chicago. Aurora's suite provided prime display space for two basic layouts: one, a simple oval; the other integrated into an HO train layout to demonstrate compatibility. Hobbyshop distributors and big chain-store buyers loved it. Moreover, the children of industry leaders went crazy over it—however, not exactly as Shikes and Giammarino had intended. Kids raced the oval-track cars so fast they spun out. The HO train system provided interest only in its potential for car-and-train wrecks.

When HIAA ended, Sylvan Sidney, editor of the trade journal *Craft, Model and Hobby Industry,* wrote, "I may be wrong, but the most exciting new product displayed at the Chicago show was Aurora's 'Highways,' an HO scale highway system that can be used in conjunction with HO trains, or used as a 'Highway' race track." Aurora took out a full page ad in the March 1960 toy industry journal *Playthings*: "An unbelievable new product destined to take its place among the best-selling items of all time!"—a claim that proved prophetic.

Back in West Hempstead, frenzied activity filled Aurora executive offices. The first issue to be resolved was the question of how the product would be marketed. Robinette and some Aurora staff thought it best to emphasize the HO automobiles as an add-on to model train layouts. Aurora's hyperactive advertising manager Donald "Bill" Silverstein led the faction that wanted to pitch slot cars as racers.

Backed by Joe Giammarino, Bill Silverstein won the day. Advertising and packaging would show racing scenes with an insert depicting the HO railroading tie-in. Silverstein prevailed on another point, as well; the "Highways" name was dropped after being deemed inappropriate for a racing set. The name that would come to define the toy segment—Model Motoring—was born.

Tooling up

Aurora's next hurdle was production. The items displayed at HIAA were either borrowed from Playcraft or handbuilt prototypes. Aurora had taken orders for tens of thousands of sets and promised September delivery, but had yet to produce their first car or section of track. And the clock was ticking.

Crafco's leased tooling was immediately shipped from Mettoy to the United States, but was declared unsuitable by Aurora's perfectionist chief engineer Joe Giammarino. Aurora production chief Frank Carver remembers being called into Giammarino's office and told that Aurora would have to cut its own tooling, as well as set up the whole

The first vibrators: Jaguar XK140 convertible (1541), Mercedes-Benz 300SL convertible (1542), Chevrolet Corvette convertible (1543), Ford Thunderbird hardtop (1544), Jag XK140 coupe (1545) and Mercedes 300SL coupe (1546), Corvette coupe (1547), Ford Galaxie Sunliner (1548, including factory-built motorless floor toy), and Galaxie 500 hardtop (1549).

manufacturing and assembly apparatus. "We'll give it a shot," replied the overwhelmed Carver.

The Aurora workday stretched from 7 a.m. to 10 p.m. and into the weekend. Joe Giammarino labored around the clock, taking catnaps in his office and living on black coffee. He remembers it as "quite a push." Aurora chief machinist Victor Kowalski re-engineered the Crafco die-cast chassis tool. His design was so good that Aurora's version was exported to Great Britain for use by Playcraft, which explains why period examples of Playcraft cars are found today with two chassis variations.

Aurora cut body tools with four cavities to quadruple production. Giammarino and Carver set up the assembly line; 30 Aurora workers were trained to bring slot car components together seamlessly. Near the end of the line assembled cars were placed on electrified track and zipped to final packaging. The West Hempstead firm's herculean effort paid off; by September Aurora began shipping the first of what would become 100,000 sets to department stores and hobby distributors. It was the beginning of something very big.

Television: Aurora's best friend

Slot cars were still an entirely new concept to mainstream American toy consumers. Model trains—yes. Mechanical cars—of course. But electric cars racing around plastic roadways?

To build consumer awareness for the new Aurora product line, Silverstein initiated advertising campaigns in popular national magazines. His reason for magazines: adult buyers would see Aurora's promotional efforts and respond at Christmas with racing sets for their children. A full-page piece in the November 3 *New York Times* said it all: "The Most Exciting New Hobby Sport Since Electric Trains."

More important, Silverstein caught the imagination of popular TV personalities with Aurora's toy racers. Carl Robinette had been right about one thing—Aurora couldn't afford TV advertising. Bill Silverstein didn't let that stop him; he actually charmed free time out of the networks. Dave Garroway, avid car buff and host of NBC's *Today,* invited Silverstein to a ten-lap, figure-eight race in his NBC offices; Garroway won. Two days later the newly confirmed slot car enthusiast devoted ten minutes on *Today* to races between himself and world-class Grand Prix racers Sterling Moss, Oliver Gendenbien, and Joakim Bonnier. Later that month Aurora slot cars appeared on the *Jack Paar Show.*

Perhaps most significant was the fact that each of these programs targeted adult viewers. Silverstein knew Aurora sets would be purchased by adults, and his entire market program—print, television, and public events—focused on this most important demographic group.

This launch-era store banner beckoned kids to the new magic of slot cars.

The early set packaging featured this depiction of Corvette vs. Jag XK140.

Ensnare the parents, went Aurora's logic, and purchase price would never be a problem.

Product launch—sort of

Aurora introduced Model Motoring in the fall of 1960 with four sets: the 1502 set at $16.95, the 1503 set at $24.95; and two uncataloged sets, one of which sold for only $10.95. Aurora production chief Frank Carver: "It hit the market and went right off the shelves. Nobody had ever seen anything like it before." Hobby-shop consumers fought over sets and telephoned stores 30 miles away to reserve a set. Bill Silverstein declared, "It was the biggest Christmas gift at the time."

Slot cars, of course, were an entirely new product, and many buyers had little idea what they were purchasing. December 26, 1960, brought that point home for Aurora—it was a day of complete pandemonium at the West Hempstead factory. Silverstein recalled there was a "tremendous" line of people outside the front doors clamoring to get in. Their cry: "This darn car won't run! Will you please sell me two more?"

Aurora staff immediately set up a "repair shop" in the lobby to show people how to make the vibrator cars work. Joanna Cuomo (daughter of Aurora's sales manager) and Frank Carver's daughter Jane ran the repair tables. The scene was repeated at Polk's Manhattan store and in hobby shops across the land; people had trouble making the slot cars run, but they loved them anyway—and they wanted to buy more. Experiencing this level of immediate devotion wasn't lost on Aurora management. "We realized we had something tremendous," said Carver.

Part of the success was novelty—the cars were completely new to American toy consumers. However, imaginative packaging and promotion also contributed to the initial groundswell. In February and March of 1961, Kellogg's Corn Flakes packaging carried the Aurora Model Motoring logo on the front and rules for a contest to win free race sets on back. The effect: millions of kids across America learned of Aurora Model Motoring at the breakfast table.

Even Kellogg's helped Model Motoring get off to a good start.

Aurora soon learned that the real profit from their fledgling product line would come not only with the initial set purchase but also with follow-up sales of separate-sale cars, add-on track items, and racing accessories. Though there was the expected rush of imitators soon after Model Motoring's launch, Aurora's competitors simply didn't have the variety the West Hempstead manufacturer offered. Aurora was out in front and pulling away quickly.

Challenges

Success, like so many other things in life, was tempered by reality. Aurora struggled with Model Motoring's biggest drawback, the vibrator motor. Although it probably could achieve its advertised top speed of 150 scale miles per hour, the vibrator motor was a temperamental little machine. Indeed, factory tests had revealed many opportunities for things to go wrong. Any dust on the track or dirt or carbonizing on contact points short-circuited the system. Ray Haines, chief of plastic kit development, discovered this problem when he took an Aurora factory race display to a Lime Rock, Connecticut, sports car rally. The cars worked fine until the real cars started racing. Dust kicked up and the Aurora slot cars shut down.

The source of the problem: the vibrator motor's actuator reed had to be adjusted just right. The first time an excited kid grabbed a car off the track, the reed or pickup shoes would bend and cause a malfunction. And with the excitement of slot car racing, this was a problem that was more than just common.

As a man whose job involved making lemonade from lemons, Bill Silverstein began turning this negative into a positive. He promoted the vibrator motor as something to be souped-up, just like the real thing. Privately he confessed, "You had to tinker with it or the bloody thing wouldn't work." Of course, all the other manufacturers jumping into the slot car business had similar problems—only their dilemmas were often worse.

A partial solution came from Rich Palmer and Dick Schwarzchild of R & R Analysis, a hobby industry consulting firm. Schwarzchild operated a Kingston, Pennsylvania, hobby shop and had experienced the flood of returns after Christmas 1960. A blunt-spoken man, Schwarzchild considered the vibrator car "a terrible product." Palmer ran Rich's Hobbytowne and Tri-O-Rama Field

Hop Up Kits, from early (front center), to AFX. Also, the Pit Kit.

The Ford Country Squire wagon (1550), Ford F-100 pickup (1551), Ford Galaxie police car (1552), Hot Rod (1553, 1554 coupe), International Semi tractor (1580, pulling van body trailer (1585) and box-body trailer (1584), Mack dump truck (1582), and 6-Wheel Mack stake truck (1583).

in Parsippany, New Jersey. Rich had also sold out Aurora slot sets, but experienced 50 percent returns after the holiday selling season.

To handle the returns, Palmer set up a repair shop and staffed it with local kids. "Adults would come in and say 'I can't make this work.' So a ten-year-old would open it up, and two seconds later away it would go." Palmer noted how the boys fiddled with the cars. From these observations he and Schwarzchild envisioned the "Hop Up Kit," a slot car accessory filled with tools, additional equipment, and a booklet of helpful hints.

They took the idea to Joe Giammarino and Derek Brand, who was dividing his time between California and West Hempstead. The four men worked out the details. Palmer wanted to include a pick-up shoe adjuster—a small screwdriver with the end sawed off and a slot cut in the end. (Lionel sold a similar tool for working on locomotive motors.) Joe Giammarino argued against the tool, citing cost and the fact that bends in the pick-ups and reed could be made without it.

Palmer won, and the adjusting tool went into the Hop Up Kit. Also included was a screwdriver, strips of fine sandpaper for cleaning the coil contact point, four oversized tires, track cleaner (an eraser), decal sheet, and "Hop-Up Hints" booklet. The Hop Up Kit sold for 98 cents and instantly became one of Aurora's most popular products; equally important, it bought Aurora precious development time in the pursuit of a new motor design for its growing slot car product line.

Always stylish, always contemporary

From the beginning of its involvement in slot cars, Aurora devoted plenty of attention to Model Motoring body styles. Aurora management believed that a wide variety would promote sets and subsequent car sales. At a time when other companies could offer only two to four body styles, Aurora introduced one new car after another. By 1962—barely two years after launch—there were 19 cars and trucks in the Model Motoring line. Competitors simply could not match Aurora's pace.

Aurora inherited the first two Model Motoring cars from Playcraft: the 1541 Jaguar and 1542 Mercedes. The Chevrolet Impala was not continued because its body had too many parts for easy assembly. To enhance the American appeal of Model Motoring, Aurora added a Chevrolet Corvette convertible (1543) and Ford Thunderbird (1544)—the first models to be designed entirely in-house.

Interestingly, the plastic used in the vibrator cars wasn't regular styrene but rather cycolac (ABS), a substance that could withstand the heat generated by the motor. Cycolac is the same material used in period telephone casings, so early Model Motoring cars often resemble phone colors of the day. This explains Aurora's turquoise cars; it was a popular early-1960s hue for kitchen phones. Black, of course,

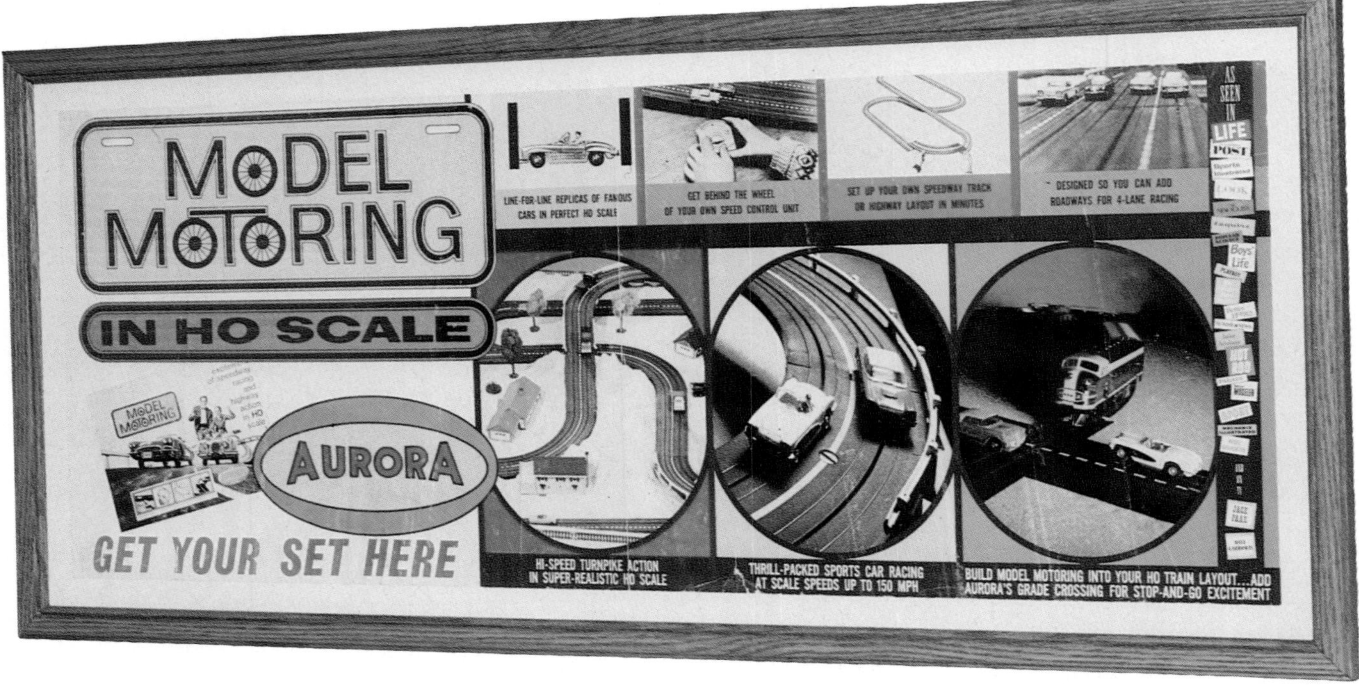

This in-store banner included the Race-Road-Rail theme.

was available, but Aurora made few in this color because they didn't show up well against black track.

Model Motoring sets came with a power controller (1533) similar to the original Playcraft version. The main changes were color and composition (from green-painted metal to gray ABS) and elimination of the ignition key. Like the cars, the controllers heated up. The tiny steering wheel speed control enhanced the illusion that you were driving a car, but in the excitement of a race the wheel tended to snap off—a definite party-ender for most kids.

The runaway success of Model Motoring created a monstrous demand for roadway track. Aurora manufactured sections by the millions, and feeding the molding machines with raw plastic became a major problem. As a short-term solution, Aurora jobbed out a substantial portion of track production to New York-area molding shops. But still the matter of sourcing enough material remained. Because of Aurora's huge appetite for plastic, Abe Shikes negotiated with suppliers across the country for inexpensive materials. His solution: combine recycled plastic—which Carver deemed "garbage"—with fresh raw plastic, color everything black, and start the machines. Joe Giammarino constantly objected to the low-grade material, arguing that quality be maintained. Out of their debate emerged "track black," an industrywide standard for roadway-grade plastic.

In the early years Aurora track was difficult to assemble. The instruction sheet even depicted three hands putting the track together! Still, Aurora's selection of track sections was unparalleled in the toy industry. Perhaps most useful was the "crisscross," which alternated cars between lanes, eliminating the need for a figure eight and overpass to make lane distance equal between the two competing cars. This kind of simple innovation kept Aurora sets well ahead of the competition.

The train tie-in

Although Aurora marketed slot cars primarily as racers, the company retained interest in the model railroad market. The first Model Motoring instruction manuals suggested a model railroading tie-in: "If you've already got an HO railroad system, Model Motoring in HO scale can be worked into it without any trouble at all. Just imagine how great it will be to have real cars and trucks barreling down real roads!" The railroad crossing section (1522) made it possible to fully integrate car and train systems.

Parkway Industries of Cleveland, Ohio, took the concept one step further. They packaged Aurora slot cars and Tyco trains together in a "Race-Road-Rail" set, available from 1961 to 1963. The set retailed for $60—a steep price for a hybrid product—and included Aurora Thunderbird and Corvette cars along with a Tyco Santa Fe diesel and three cars. The potential for train-auto wrecks was highlighted in ads—certainly not the ultimate in decorum, but definitely a tip of the hat to what children would be doing with their Race-Road-Rail sets.

Aurora had been making plastic model house kits for HO railroading since the late 1950s. Offering structures appropriate to racing seemed natural, beginning with the 658 Service Station, a Texaco gas station complete with a billboard proclaiming it a "Model Motoring Service

Model Motoring structure kits made many a slot raceway more respectable.

Center." However, once it became clear model railroaders were more interested in trains, Aurora discontinued the Service Station.

However, building kits for slot cars was still a valid concept—Aurora simply needed better inspiration. In 1963 it announced nine new Model Motoring kits, including four that were never issued (hay bales and hedges, billboard and signs, hot dog stand, and trophy presentation platform). Of the five kits produced, the Start-Finish Pylons (1450) seems to have been least popular. The Double Station Pit Stop (1453) was continually in demand, since kids considered it a good spot to park their extra cars. The Curved Bleachers (1456) fit the outside radius of Aurora's curved track perfectly. Kids across America spent their savings on these add-ons, boosting Aurora's profits.

The Grand National

Hobby industry consultant Rich Palmer came up with his greatest contribution to slot cars in 1961: in-store racing championships. Throughout the summer he conducted six weekly races featuring Aurora cars exclusively. As part of his routine, he sent a newsletter to Aurora headquarters.

Silverstein paged through one of Palmer's newsletters one day and caught the mention of the Aurora races. He sent his assistant Shirley Henshel to Palmer's store on a fact-finding mission, and her visit paid two dividends. First, she convinced *Look* Magazine to do a story on slot car races (July 3, 1962). More important, Silverstein used Palmer's event as inspiration for Aurora's own series of sponsored hobbyshop races. He hired Palmer as a consultant for $50 a month ("Enough to pay for your hockey tickets," said Silverstein) and began planning what would become the Grand National.

Starting in October 1961, Palmer and four other retailers conducted test competitions. The following month Palmer took several Aurora cars modified by his most successful racers and showed them on the *Today* show. NBC's John Chancellor maneuvered the cars around the road and model railroad course with only one car-train collision.

Following the success of the trial races, Aurora announced plans for a national racing program. Silverstein declared, "I think we're onto something big." He traveled to Detroit to enlist Ford Motor Corporation as co-sponsor. "This was a hard sell, because not only did I want to use their name—I wanted $100,000 a year from them." He spent the day being passed from one department

The Pit Palace, a never-produced landmark on the Model Motoring landscape

to another—advertising, marketing, youth division, public relations. "Finally they sat me down and said they have a guy coming in. So he walked in, put his feet on the desk, and said, 'All right, talk for five minutes.'" Silverstein pitched, and the Ford executive smiled. "I love it; it's a go." The guy with his feet on the desk—Lee Iacocca, father of the Ford Mustang and the Ford-Aurora Grand National.

Silverstein instructed Palmer and Schwarzchild to design a program the average shopkeeper could run without undue disruption to store routine. The result was a nine-week series requiring only two hours a week. Palmer designed a standard race course with one long straightaway and a three-curve backstretch.

A rare pre-Thunderjets store "racing center" tin sign

An impressive award for the winner of the 1962 Grand National.

The design rewarded kids who could soup-up their cars and those who could steer through tight curves. Palmer named it the "Mille Miglia" after the famous Italian "thousand mile" auto race.

Aware that summer months are traditionally slow for hobby retailers, Aurora scheduled races for June and July. Race packets included a rule book, two trophies, window streamers, pennants, Ford "406" decals—which racers were required to stick on their cars—score sheets, and Model Motoring club cards. Although Aurora later claimed that 5,000 stores took part in the Grand National, Palmer estimated the actual number at 500. Still, the Grand National was the most innovative store promotion to date.

Aurora kept the competition keen. And because of their deep-pocketed sponsor, it remained exclusively Ford.

- Only five cars could be used—the Galaxie 500 Sunliner, Galaxie 500 Club Victoria, Country Squire Station Wagon, Ford F-100 pickup, and the Police Car (1548 through 1552). (As it turned out, the Sunliner convertible was the most successful racer, because of its low center of gravity.)
- Race contestants could tune the vibrator motor
- Two local celebrity witnesses certified the official time
- Forty-eight state winners were culled from all store winners
- Eight regional competitions determined the eight finalists who went to New York.

Toots Shors' Restaurant in New York City hosted the preliminary finals on August 20, 1962. It included three races: a 40-foot drag strip (20 percent of the total point value); twisting rally course with one full stop (30 percent); and the Mille Miglia course (50 percent).

The leader after one day of competition was Henry Harnish, the teen who began his career by winning at Palmer's store. Palmer declared Harnish had received no favors. "This kid has nerves of steel," explained Palmer. While the pressure got to other racers, Harnish's hands were rock-solid.

The final race was featured on the next morning's *Today* show. Young Henry dominated, lapping the other three finalists in a 20-lap Mille Miglia race. Ford offered a new 1962 Thunderbird as grand prize—or a raincheck for one when Henry turned 21. Henry's father took the T-Bird on the spot.

Aurora slot cars were becoming part of the American toy-buying consciousness—and the best was yet to come.

2

THUNDERJETS

the new generation

Early Thunderjet 500 packaging—now the race was between T-Bird and XKE, a match straight out of California surf pop.

In 1962 slot car mania swept the country. Trade journals reported sales of model railroad items down; slot manufacturers couldn't keep pace with demand. "Frankly," said one retailer, "racing cars overpower everything else we sell." More than 20 companies marketed slot car sets in 1962, but most of them sold the larger 1/32 or 1/24 scale sets. Aurora did have competition in HO, however: Atlas, Lionel, Marx, and Tyco—all model train manufacturers, to one degree or another, attempting to diversify in the face of stiff slot car competition. Derek Brand considered Marx Aurora's best challenger. The toy industry's value-pricing leader had developed a small DC motor that worked well and was inexpensive. Still, Marx cars sold for $3.95 at a time when Aurora's sold for $2.49—an obvious burden for the frugal

Early Thunderjets: Ford Galaxie convertible (1351), Ford Galaxie hardtop (1352), Ford Falcon hardtop (1354), Thunderbird convertible (1355), Chevy Corvette Stingray (1356), Buick Riviera (1357), Jaguar XKE (1358), and Ford Fairlane hardtop (1353).

Marx marketeers to bear. Perhaps most important to kids was the simple fact that Aurora cars were faster.

Aurora outsold Marx and all other HO producers combined. Polls revealed that virtually all hobby retailers stocked Aurora slot car products—an astounding fact and strong testimony to Aurora's dominance in the marketplace. Strombecker (maker of 1/32 and 1/24 cars) was a distant second, with Atlas, Scalextric (1/30), and Tyco trailing. Good times just kept getting better for Aurora.

The Thunderjet 500

Despite its commanding lead, Aurora understood that slot cars were a rapidly evolving product. Intense competition would ultimately expose the weak link in Aurora's system—the vibrator motor. Even Brand felt his creation was "not a very good motor." In addition to mechanical shortcomings, the AC-powered vibrator played havoc with television reception—not a popular trait with parents.

Aurora marketing maven Bill Silverstein and the Hop Up Kits had bought the necessary time for Derek Brand to develop the next-generation power plant for Aurora slot cars. Brand thought he'd found the answer: a new DC motor with two fixed magnets and a conventional armature. He built his prototype at Crafco using magnets he ground into shape by hand, electrical contacts from a washing machine, and a commutator made with a Formica chip pried from his desktop. He packaged the prototype in a car and airmailed it to West Hempstead for inspection. One of the R&D team members placed the car on a standard Aurora vibrator layout and instantly burned up the DC motor with alternating current. Aurora R&D staff didn't grasp what had happened—something of an interesting commentary in itself—and simply mailed the dead motor back to Crafco's California workshop.

Derek Brand saw the burnt armature and immediately knew what had happened. He got the motor working again and planned another showing for Aurora management. On his next New York visit, the subject of the new motor came up as Brand and sales director John Cuomo fished off Long Island. Cuomo mentioned that retailers were still complaining about the vibrator motor, and Brand said he had the solution in his suitcase.

This time Brand was in charge when his prototype was tested, and the results were quite different. Joe Giammarino was pleased. He later declared, "He was quite a guy, that Derek Brand. I liked him a lot. When I first saw him I said, 'You've got to come to work for me.'" Giammarino, the no-nonsense engineer, had found a kindred spirit.

Joe Giammarino contacted Carl Robinette and proclaimed that Derek Brand's talents could be put to better use in New York. Robinette agreed, and the Anglo-Californian moved from Santa Barbara to West Hempstead.

Brand established a Model Motoring lab upstairs at the factory, across the hall from Giammarino's office. There he and ten assistants developed new track sections, electrical components, and patterns for car bodies from eight in the morning until seven-thirty at night.

Derek Brand and Joe Giammarino immediately set about bringing the new motor into production. Brand did most of the design, but Giammarino was a man of strong opinions and plenty of manufacturing experience. Production manager Frank Carver tracked down sources for components, going as far as Switzerland to find good-quality gears.

The new motor design was innovative and worthy of a patent. At first Aurora's attorney was skeptical, but he succeeded in getting a patent for the new engine. The names of Brand and Giammarino were assigned to patent number 3,243,917.

The result was best summarized by Aurora advertising: "A new miracle motor . . . it will outperform every other slot-car motor on the market, by any standard you can dream up." In a stroke of brand-concepting brilliance, Silverstein named it the "Thunderjet 500." The hype continued: "Laboratory tests prove a Model Motoring car with a T-jet 500 under the hood will exceed the speed of sound in scale miles per hour." Who could resist such a claim?

No one, as it turned out. Aurora unveiled the Thunderjet 500 motor at the 1963 HIAA convention and it was the hit of the show—except with Aurora's competitors. The T-jet was twice as fast as the vibrator, nearly three times as fast as Marx, more than twice as fast as Tyco, and about 30 percent faster than Aurora's nearest competitor, Atlas. (Faller of Germany quickly copied the T-jet, and in Brand's opinion, "did a fine job." Aurora agreed not to sue Faller as long as they kept their product out of the United States market.) Jose Rodriguez, Jr., reviewing the Thunderjet 500 for *Car Model* magazine (July 1963) declared it the best motor he'd ever seen. Derek Brand had once again delivered a knockout punch for Aurora.

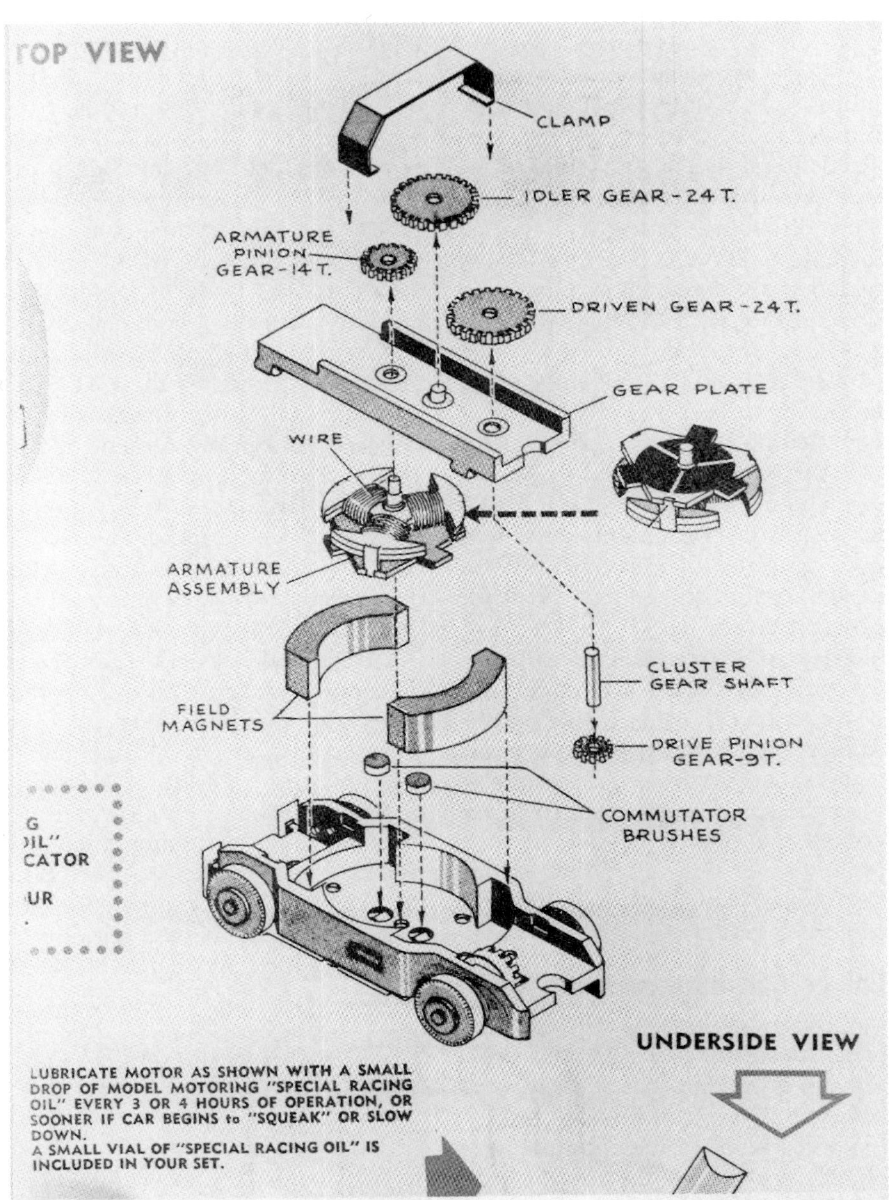

Aurora's instruction manuals depicted the T-jet in all its exploded-view glory.

Innovation in design

The most obvious innovation was the Thunderjet 500's design. A conventional motor employs a rotating armature and magnets encased in a metal can. Competitors mounted their motors horizontally—on the motor's side—so that the motor drive shaft extending outward would drive the rear-axle gear, propelling the car forward.

The Thunderjet took that concept and turned it on its end—literally. The T-jet motor sat upright in the chassis. Its drive shaft extended from the top of the motor, giving it a flattened look Brand dubbed the "pancake." This lowered the car's center of gravity and added an even greater performance advantage.

The T-jet's drive train was also a complete departure from standard slot car design. While a typical can motor transferred power with a simple two-gear arrangement, the T-jet required a five-gear linkage to deliver power from the drive shaft, across the top of the motor, and down to the rear axle. It sounds complicated, but it was actually quite simple and extremely effective.

There were many more-subtle innovations within the Thunderjet, but the most obvious was its oversized armature. Since it was clear slot cars would not play a part in HO railroading, Brand was free to increase motor size. The chassis was widened and lengthened. Cars were now closer to 1/80 than 1/87 in scale, but everyone agreed it was a positive change: the cars were easier to assemble and better for hobbyist tinkering.

Aurora also enlarged the steering wheel controller to make it easier to handle. Designers added two new features: a direction-reverse switch and a "brake" that cut track power. Racers like Henry Harnish discovered that the brake was better for slowing at curves than turning down power. Kids who raced Aurora cars and used Aurora controllers had an obvious advantage over their competitors, and Aurora advertising of the day drove that point home, time and time again. You either raced Aurora, or you came in second.

End of the vibrating road

The debut of Thunderjets meant death for vibrators. Old stock remained in stores for a while, and some hobbyists still enjoyed tinkering with them. However, after production of a million and a half copies, vibrator mechanisms were soon history. And because vibrator car bodies were too small for the larger T-jet chassis, all but four were discontinued. The survivors through modification: Hot Rods (1553 and 1554) and the Mack Dump and Stake Truck (1582 and 1583). Aurora also converted the International Semi (1580) into a tow truck (1364).

The four vibrator holdovers joined Aurora's growing stable of new Thunderjet models. It seems amazing in today's market-research-dominated world of toy manufacture, but in the early 1960s, selecting new cars for Model Motoring hinged completely on the humble preferences of Derek Brand and his R&D team. They used photographs supplied by auto manufacturers (especially Ford) and photographs from car magazines. Draftsmen then produced engineering drawings from which Brand carved his body prototypes. He shaped his patterns in sugar pine three times the size of the actual HO body. It took only a week to complete a body design.

Aurora relied on outside toolmakers to produce their slot car body molds. More often than not, finished patterns were sent to Ace Tool & Die in Newark, New Jersey, where a large quantity of Aurora steel production molds were cut. When complete, the tools were delivered to West Hempstead and production commenced.

Meanwhile, Derek Brand was only one man, and Aurora needed more automotive variety than he alone could design. To enhance development, Aurora occasionally turned to HMS, a Willow Grove, Pennsylvania, company that designed Aurora model kits, including the now-classic monster figure kits. HMS technicians carved patterns in acetate, a medium that is easier to use than wood but less stable. Interestingly, HMS generally carved its patterns in HO scale, a practice that limited detail.

HMS patterns went to Ferriot Brothers in Toledo, Ohio, for tool cutting. Ferriot manufactured Aurora figure kit tooling as well as molds for Marx playset figures. Unlike the cut-steel molds produced by Ace, Ferriot produced tooling by the lost-wax method in beryllium copper alloy. The result: a quicker and less expensive process for Aurora.

Production, of course, was concentrated at West Hempstead. At first Aurora's standard molding machines did all the work, producing bodies from four-cavity molds. However, after a few years Giammarino switched to smaller German-made Arburg machines. The Arburgs molded only one body at a time, but they were fully automated; one worker could tend several machines, and, in Joe Giammarino's words, they "went like jackrabbits."

The magic of Aurora marketing

On the marketing front, Aurora went to the real racing world for Model

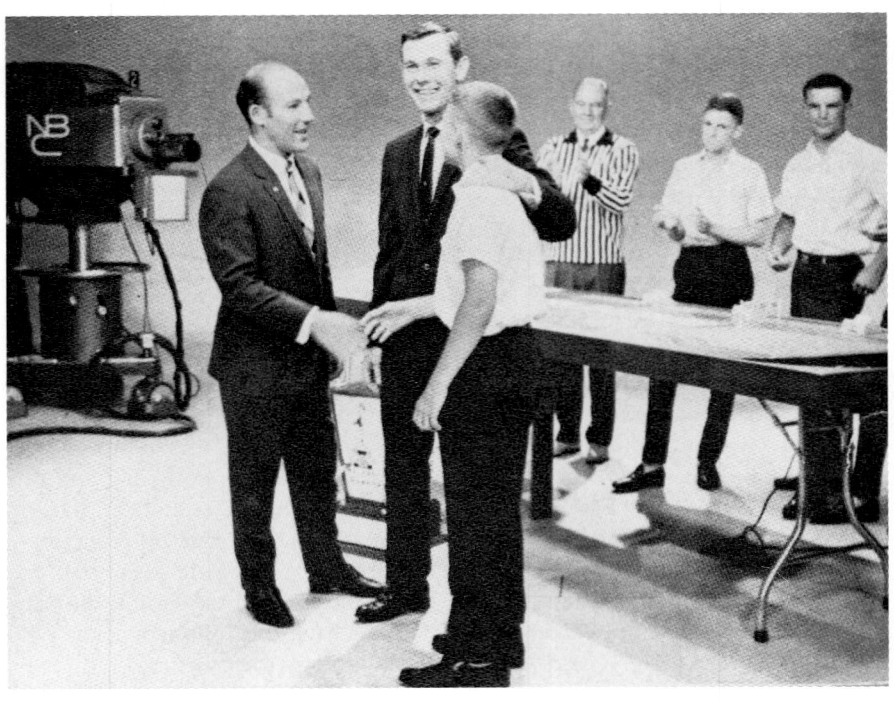

Sterling Moss (left) congratulates 1963 Grand National champ Ronnie Colerick as the *Tonight Show*'s Johnny Carson jokes with the audience. Photo courtesy *Rod & Custom Models*.

Indianapolis racers in regular (1359) as well as silver and gold chrome (1360). Also, Grand Prix racer (1361), along with members of the venerable families Mack and International: Mack dump (1362), Mack stake (1363), and some interesting variations of the long-lived Mack wrecker (1364).

Motoring's first spokesman—former world champion Grand Prix driver Sterling Moss. As Bill Silverstein felt, what better presentation could Aurora make to kids across America—and to their parents' wallets—than a heroic racing hero?

Overnight, Sterling Moss' photo graced the cover of Aurora's Model Motoring catalog, and he served as Chief Steward of the Second Ford-Aurora Grand National Model Motoring Championship. Silverstein knew the racer's winning personality matched his winning ways on the circuit. He also had one other important qualification—he was retired and available for full-time representation. Silverstein didn't want his spokesman killed in a racing accident.

Aurora retained the same basic format for the Second Grand Nationals. Changes enhanced the competition: Aurora added two more trophies to the dealer race package and included a cardboard "Used Car Lot" display. The idea was for dealers to take old cars as partial payment for new ones, then resell the old cars to enthusiasts. Entrants received a "427" car decal. The final change: the eight national finalists were selected from time trials, eliminating regional competitions and the need for contestant travel.

The Grand National finals were staged in the Mercury Ballroom of the New York Hilton, with more than 200 spectators watching the action on the three drag, rally, and Mille Miglia tracks. True to his new role, Sterling Moss mingled with the crowd; *Car Model* magazine's L. T. Shaw (November 1963) found him "a warm, friendly man, intensely interested in all aspects of the contest and extremely easy to talk to." (Silverstein's magic was working.) Shaw also noted the crowd's enthusiasm: "I overheard one boy's mother explain the differences between vibrator motors and the new Thunderjet 500 to a curious bystander as calmly (and correctly) as if she were discussing a cake recipe."

The four best drivers appeared on the August 20 Tonight show. The slowest qualifier was twelve-year-old Ronnie Colerick of Rapid City, South Dakota, who was assigned lane one after the other drivers had picked their lanes. The race started with wild spinouts by all four drivers, but Colerick settled down and pulled away from the other boys. The race became a runaway when the others were pressed into mistakes while trying to catch up.

Colerick explained that he was less affected by the pressure of the televised race because he was too young to appreciate what was at stake. His dad owned a hobby shop, and Ronnie had spent up to five hours a day honing his driving skills. When Carson presented Colerick with his trophy and 1963 Ford Thunderbird, Ronnie exclaimed "Neat, man! I'll let my dad drive it sometimes." Host Johnny Carson quipped, "You mean he wins a Thunderbird for that?!"

The need for standards

Slot car racing's popularity was growing beyond the basic home

Hot Rod roadster (1365) and coupe (1366) on the track. On the right: Maserati (1367), with and without stripe, and Ferrari GTO (1368). On the left: classic Lincoln Continental (1369) and AC Cobra (1370) with pre-production test shot of the body in translucent plastic.

road racing set. Aurora's Grand National was nationally known, and competitions sponsored by other manufacturers, clubs, and model car magazines vied for attention. While the vast majority of racing sets were sold for home use by kids, a growing number of hobbyists were transforming slot racing into a sport. Aurora president Abe Shikes saw this as another potential market. Consultants Rich Palmer and Dick Schwarzchild approached Shikes with the idea of founding a national slot racing association.

Abe Shikes supported the concept. The result: the Miniature International Racing Association (MINRA). Naturally, Aurora's connection was kept secret. Shikes put up $20,000 to launch the organization but left operations to his consultants. Initially, MINRA's official headquarters was in Englewood, New Jersey, but after a few months it was moved to an office in Palmer's store. Homer Hleovas (or Leovas, as he spelled his name for public purposes), well-known Sports Car Club of America driver and officer, was named executive director.

Like any sanctioning association, MINRA's mission was to establish order and uniformity to the infant sport of slot car racing. Before MINRA, each manufacturer and racing organization set its own standards and made its own rules. The result was chaos. For the sport to grow, it needed a national organization. MINRA, Aurora hoped, would be that organization.

At the 1963 HIAA national convention Homer Leovas spoke about MINRA, and Aurora's John Cuomo, chairman of the HIAA slot car committee, urged hobby shops to set up race centers along MINRA guidelines. Leovas said MINRA would produce a rule book setting standards for layouts, race management, and car classifications. It would also begin publishing *In the Groove,* a newsletter for the slot car community. MINRA would supply mail-order trophies and other items necessary for a top-quality race. MINRA members would receive *In the Groove,* membership card, and club pin. It was a well-formed concept that deserved support.

In the Groove's first issue appeared in February 1963. Considering its hidden benefactor, the newspaper was remarkably evenhanded in its treatment of manufacturers other than Aurora. MINRA sponsored its first national championship race—a drag—at Schwarzchild's Kingston, Pennsylvania, shop. Unlike Aurora's Grand Nationals, there was a twist: competitors mailed their cars to Schwarzchild's shop, where they were raced by MINRA's team of experienced slot

The ill-fated Beat the Champ competition had all the makings of a surefire promotional winner.

FAMOUS RACING DRIVER
GLENN "FIREBALL" ROBERTS
SAYS

IF YOU CAN BEAT MY TIME ON THE MODEL MOTORING LAYOUT IN YOUR LOCAL HOBBY SHOP YOU MIGHT WIN THIS GREAT NEW FORD MUSTANG !!

EVERYBODY CAN WIN A PRIZE IN THE EXCITING NEW FORD-AURORA CONTEST!

"BEAT THE CHAMP!"

HI, FIREBALL! I'M RARIN' TO GO!

GREAT, TOMMY! THIS HOBBY SHOP IS WHERE WE START!

ALL YOU HAVE TO DO IS BUY ONE OF THESE NEW AURORA MODEL MOTORING CARS AND RACE AGAINST THE CLOCK!

HEY, THAT SOUNDS EASY! IMAGINE ME BEATING THE FIREBALL'S TIME!

AND IF YOU DO, YOU'LL GET ONE OF THESE MUSTANG AWARD PINS!

THEN EVERY-BODY'LL KNOW I "BEAT THE CHAMP"!

RIGHT! AND IF YOU'RE A STORE WINNER, YOU CAN GO ON TO COMPETE FOR THE REAL FORD!

WOW! MAYBE I'LL BE THE MODEL MOTORING CHAMPION OF 1964!

EVERYBODY'S GOT A CHANCE IN THIS TERRIFIC RACING COMPETITION! VISIT YOUR LOCAL HOBBY SHOP AND GET ALL THE DETAILS! MAY 1st. IS THE STARTING DATE!

MODEL MOTORING

AURORA

AURORA PLASTICS CORP., WEST HEMPSTEAD, N.Y.

Kids who could beat Fireball Roberts' time would have earned a gold-plated stop-watch/Mustang pin.

racers. The fastest car was Gene Wagner's HO Thunderjet-powered Corvette, which covered the scale half-mile in just 2.451 seconds—820 scale miles per hour. Aurora was so pleased it reported the accomplishment in its 1964 catalog.

Beat the Champ

All good things get a little weary with repetition, so Aurora changed course for 1964's Third Annual Ford-Aurora Grand Nationals. Many hobby dealers had lost their enthusiasm for in-store racing, but Aurora's Bill Silverstein was undaunted. He developed Beat the Champ, an in-store racing concept that featured an 18" x 66" oval based on Ford's Dearborn, Michigan, test track.

Silverstein's plan was simple: time a real-life race car driver's performance on the oval, then encourage kids around the country to beat the champ's time on their local hobby shop's track. Those who did received gold-plated Ford Mustang pins. The contest would last only two weeks, and the finalists would be the seven fastest regional qualifiers.

Bill Silverstein selected Aurora's model of the new Ford Mustang as official car. Aurora supplied participating hobby shops with special candy-colored hardtops (1501) for use in the time trials; this and all subsequent Grand Nationals would require stock cars. One rule: the Mustangs could be tuned but not modified. The finalists would receive Aurora Mustangs upon arrival in New York, giving them just 24 hours to adjust the cars to their liking.

The previous year's Grand Nationals had featured retired racing champ Stirling Moss as Aurora's celebrity. For Beat the Champ, however, Bill Silverstein felt it necessary to have a current racing star represent the contest. To that end, he recruited NASCAR all-time money winner Glenn "Fireball" Roberts as official "champ."

Fireball flew to Dearborn to kick off Beat the Champ at a reception for Ford executives and hobby industry representatives. Following the reception, he flew to Charlotte, North Carolina, for the annual 600-mile NASCAR event. Seven minutes into the race, a car spun out ahead of Roberts. His car sideswiped another, veered into the infield, flipped, and burst into flames. A fellow driver pulled Fireball from the wreckage, but Aurora's spokesman was burned over 70 percent of his body because he had refused to wear a fireproof suit. He died five weeks later.

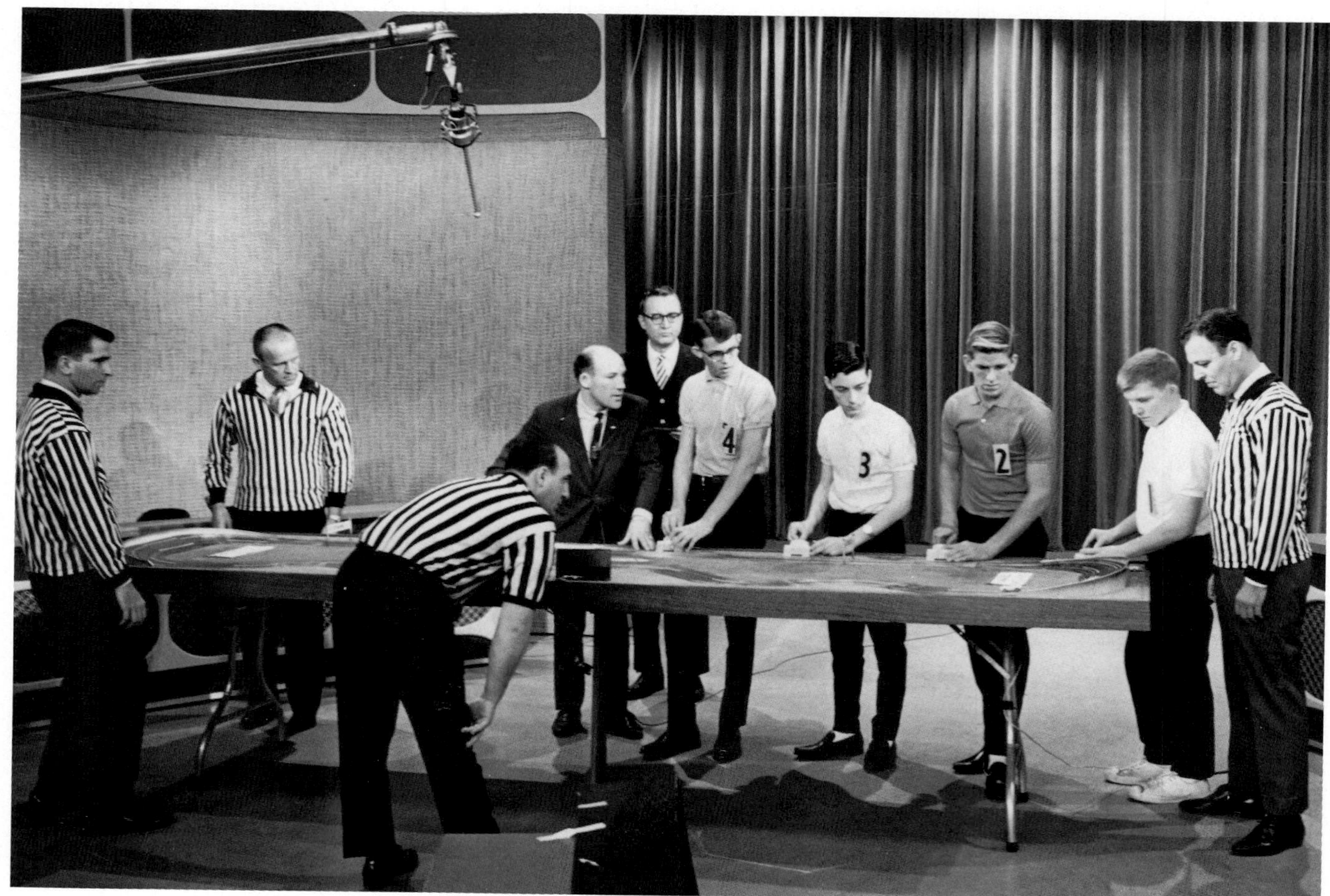

Steve Allen (center, rear) and Stirling Moss keep a watchful eye over Grand National finalists during an *I've Got a Secret* Aurora racing interlude. Tom Kilduff (no. 1) took top honors and a new Mustang.

Super Model Motoring, in all its ill-fated glory, clockwise from top: 1931 Ford pickup (1751), 1957 Thunderbird (1756), 1932 Deuce Rod (1758), 1949 Mercury coupe (1755), 1932 Ford chopped sedan (1752), 1936 Ford convertible (1753), 1927 Ford T (1757), 1957 Chevy (1754).

The accident had a chilling effect at Aurora. Immediately upon hearing of the accident, Aurora canceled Beat the Champ and terminated all publicity featuring Roberts' name. Silverstein had been right the first time when he signed Moss; retired legends don't die on race tracks in the middle of promotions.

Because of Roberts' untimely demise, Grand National time trials weren't held until early fall—and in a greatly revised format. On October 6 the fastest drivers from each state went to their local dealers for the final trial. At 4:30 Eastern Time the command "Go!" was issued via telephone from Aurora headquarters, and all forty-eight races started simultaneously. Each store had three independent timers to verify results, and Aurora required winning cars be impounded to make sure (in Palmer's words) "nobody had been Mickey Mousing around with the car."

On Sunday, November 14, the New York Hilton hosted preliminary races among seven regional winners; the next morning four finalists taped Steve Allen's *I've Got a Secret* CBS game show. The boys' secret: "One of us is going to win $5,000 tonight." Once the quiz was finished, the contestants moved to the stage where Derek Brand and his crew had set up the race course. Stirling Moss officiated. Preliminaries leader Tom Kilduff chose the outside lane and proceeded to win the final race, a new Ford Mustang, and a $2,000 college scholarship.

Super Model Motoring: the 1/48 wrong turn

Just a week after the Grand National finals, the National Custom Car Show opened in New York City. As was typical for the time, model and slot car manufacturers had booths alongside real-life cars. Aurora had big news for the automotive world: the debut of Super Model Motoring, slot cars in 1/48 scale. "Not too big . . . not too small, but sized right in between."

In basic terms, Super Model Motoring attempted to find an unoccupied niche between small HO cars and large 1/32 and 1/24 systems. Joe Giammarino hoped Lionel railroaders would support the size-compatible line. Although Super Model Motoring cars had a new, larger chassis, their motor was the same T-jet found in Aurora HO cars. Body styles designed by HMS were all in the hot rod vein: a '31 Model A pickup, '32 Ford Sedan, '36 Ford convertible, and '57 Chevy hardtop (1751 through 1754). Aurora launched Super Model Motoring

The line that never launched: Monstermobiles, slot cars based on Aurora's hybrid hot rod and monster figure kits like Frankenstein's Flivver.

Grand National Competition Pac. Three regular-issue Mustangs: convertible (1372), standard coupe (1372), and 2+2 fastback (1373); plus two candy-colored fastback shells (1501).

with two sets, one at $24.95 and the other at $29.95, complete with an overpass to construct an over-under figure eight. There were no other accessories. Given the limited variety, Aurora's entry into O gauge racing looked timid.

The hobby industry didn't know what to make of the 1/48 cars. Jose Rodriguez, Jr., of *Car Model* liked the line, but asked the immortal question, "Do we need another scale?" Others criticized the cars' lack of detail and accurate proportioning. The T-jet motor generated plenty of power, but the question remained: Who wanted them?

During 1964 Aurora added four more "rods" to the line: a 1947 Mercury, 1957 Thunderbird, 1932 Ford Deuce, and 1927 Model T rod (1755 through 1758). Sales were terrible, and Aurora let the line die quietly. "We couldn't give them away," observed Brand, who thought hot rods had limited appeal. Proving you do only live twice, Aurora disposed of its surplus inventory of 1/48 chassis by selling them to the A. C. Gilbert Company, which used them in a James Bond spy slot car set.

If only, if only . . .

The sudden death of Super Model Motoring had more impact than many today realize—the line's untimely demise kept Aurora from issuing a handful of cars that would have become certain collectors' classics today.

The cars were 1/48 scale Monstermobiles. 1964 was the year of monster mania in America. *The Addams Family* and *The Munsters* cavorted across television screens, and Aurora was selling Universal Movie Monster figure kits like crazy. Aurora R&D team members designed patterns for at least three cars driven by popular monsters: Frankenstein, Dracula, and the Wolf Man. The cars were miniature versions of popular Aurora model kits depicting monsters driving hot rods. Aurora even issued a press release announcing the cars, but never produced them. Today, photographs are all that remain of what might have been some of the most collectible slot cars ever manufactured.

Leadership

Despite the 1/48 setback, HO slot car popularity surged. By 1965 HO Model Motoring was a staple in

Mid-1960s Thunderjet set boxes featured the Ford Mustang, then America's best-selling vehicle.

Candy Colors, in early painted and later plated versions. From left: Jaguar XKE (1392), Ford GT (1395), Corvette Stingray (1391), Grand Prix racer (1393), Ferrari 250 GTO (1394), and Cobra GT (1396).

the toy and hobby industry. Indeed, the enormous popularity of slot cars had made Aurora Plastics Corporation the largest hobby company in the world—an incredible achievement in such a short period of time. The Thunderjet motor was powerful enough to keep slot enthusiasts happy and reliable enough to be a hit in the mass market. Marx and Lionel dropped out, leaving just Tyco and Atlas to compete for leftovers.

1965 wasn't a major year for innovation at Aurora. The only novel introduction was cosmetic—painting six models in brilliant "Candy Colors" (1391 through 1396). Later, Aurora would plate these same cars in candy-colored chrome. Aurora also produced some new track products, but these too were largely cosmetic.

The most spectacular new item—"Cobra Climb" Spiral Roadway Support (1594), a base and pedestal with arms that tilted curved track sections up, into a 360-degree spiral, then down.

Five other track accessories also appeared, the most interesting to serious racers being the Corner Crossover (1513). Racers had asked for this segment, because it sent cars into opposite lanes on a curve, following the path that centrifugal force would compel real cars to follow on a race course.

After the tragedy of Fireball Roberts, the 1965 Ford-Aurora Grand National returned to the weekly in-store format. Silverstein retained Dan Gurney as celebrity race marshal. Local races were conducted in June; opening rounds of the finals were staged on December 9 at Aurora's massive new Raceway Center complex in West Hempstead. There were five preliminary race courses, and for the first time, they included tracks for 1/32 and 1/25 cars. This was Aurora's track, however, and the HO races carried the most importance.

Upon completion of the opening rounds, Aurora management and the top four contestants drove

The Mike Douglas Show **hosted the 1965 Grand National finals. Terry-Thomas, Ethel Merman, and Dan Dailey watched from the set. Aurora's Rich Palmer (left) and Dick Schwarzchild served as race officials.**

to Philadelphia. The final race was held on *The Mike Douglas Show*. John Seeley of Rapid City duplicated the feat of his neighbor (and 1963 winner) Ronnie Colerick by driving a Mustang 2+2 to victory. Seeley received his trophy and keys to a real Mustang 2+2 from world land speed record-holder Craig Breedlove.

3

SCALE
battle for supremacy

The slot car boom of the 1960s is defined in two letters: HO. This one scale dominated sales and outsold larger-scale cars by a wide margin. However, HO sets were primarily the domain of the mass-market starter sets generally sold to and for children, and adult interest in slot cars was beginning to take a different turn.

As the decade progressed, manufacturers of larger-scale cars attempted to attract those adult hobbyists. Their diversification and quality enhancement programs worked: teenagers and adults discovered big slot car racing as a more challenging approach to the hobby. Large slot cars zoomed in popularity in the mid-1960s, leading to a second slot explosion—a boom that remained separate from the enduring mass appeal of HO cars.

Aurora's Dick Schwarzchild and Bill Silverstein with racing legend Carroll Shelby (right) at Aurora's raceway.

Rise of the raceway

Since larger slot layouts didn't fit in most homes, raceways were the only answer. Like so many trends, slot car parlors showed up first in California—the earliest opening in 1961 Los Angeles. Two years later, there were 30 raceways, nearly all in the Los Angeles area. And by 1964, the boom had jumped the Rocky Mountains into metropolitan centers of the Midwest and East.

Craft, Model and Hobby Industry filled its pages with articles explaining how to cash in on the raceway bonanza. An early lesson learned was that noisy raceways didn't mix with retail hobby environments. Dealers, however, could recoup the overhead of a separate facility by renting track time at 50 cents a half-hour. Most also rented cars. And raceways invariably included a kit and parts counter where racers could buy cars and supplies.

There were two kinds of raceways: bare-bones, concrete-floored facilities for serious racers and plush, carpeted "entertainment centers" for the broader casual market. Dealers soon discovered business was almost all male, with the 15-year-old boy dominating the demographic profile.

The heady, early days of slot raceways did produce some notes of caution from veteran hobby industry observers. *Craft, Model and Hobby* reminded readers of the trampoline center craze a few years earlier, warning that slot car parlors might be another "bubble." A Californian writing to *Model Car & Track* in the November 1964 issue noted, "Out here there are too many tracks. Some will live and some won't." Others contended that outside big cities, America was largely unaware of slot car racing and predicted raceway growth was only just beginning.

Aurora management felt that their leadership role in slot cars demanded they too get into the raceway business—and do it in a very big way. Aurora purchased an old Vic Tanny gym down the block from the West Hempstead factory. Dick Schwarzchild, who had been brought in-house as Bill Silverstein's sales and promotion assistant, was given the task of setting up the new raceway.

However, Schwarzchild was skeptical of the long-term success of

Aurora and K&B 1/32 cars. Back row from the left: Mustang (3253), Comet (3258), Pontiac (3252), Corvair (3254), and Barracuda (3255). Front row from the left: Chaparral (3256), Lola (3259), Ford GT (3251), and Cobra (3257).

slot raceways. He observed that average drivers spent too much time retrieving crashed cars from the floor and returning them to the track—a bad omen.

Silverstein made sure the raceway's July 22, 1965, grand opening was a national event. He assembled 40 reporters at the Manhattan Biltmore and put them on a chartered coach to West Hempstead—along with a caterer, plenty of food, and a few Broadway chorus girls. Five of the East Coast's top slot racers were on hand to demonstrate their skills. Aurora declared the Raceway Center their new proving grounds—their way of keeping fingers on the pulse of the hobby.

The reluctant Schwarzchild had done a terrific job. Nine large tracks—seven for large-scale cars, two for HO, each with color-coded lanes—filled the 16,000-square-foot center. Modern swivel chairs enhanced racers' comfort. Walls featured large photos of race cars in action. The hobby shop carried the latest cars and equipment by all major manufacturers, not just Aurora. How could it not thrive?

The move into large scale

Joe Giammarino recalled that Aurora felt obliged to get involved in the booming big-car market rather than forfeiting it to the competition. "Where we could make a buck, we'd make it," he recalled. Derek Brand added, "Revell had a 1/32 system, and we looked at it enviously and said, 'If they can do it, we can do it.'"

Bill Silverstein shared Schwarzchild's reservations about large slot cars. He felt that going into large cars diluted Aurora's commitment to HO. Indeed, it went against Model Motoring's slogan, "Twice the race in half the space." Aurora nonetheless gave its new 1/32 cars top billing at the 1965 HIAA convention.

Called Aurora Americans A-Jets, the cars were marketed like their HO counterparts—as ready-to-run cars in packaged sets for the home, not specialty cars for the slot enthusiast. Dan Gurney signed on as A-Jets spokesman. Aurora initially offered ten sports and Grand Prix body styles, all featuring large American flag stickers on their doors. The two basic sets sold for $39.95 and $49.95—quite an investment for a Christmas toy.

Interestingly, A-Jets' running gear was partly derivative, partly original. In a nod to compatibility, Aurora mounted the braided-metal pickups on either side of the guide blade, like all other 1/32 cars. It meant that A-Jets would run on anyone's track.

Originality, however, was not lacking. Aurora's aluminum chassis was a West Hempstead creation, just as the innovative Challenger sidewinder motor (3250) was. The new motor was pure Derek Brand. He took a T-jet and turned it on its side—hence, a "sidewinder."

The Challenger was larger than a T-jet and was packaged in a unique snap-together metal and plastic casing, but its three-pole armature and distinctively shaped magnets revealed T-jet heritage.

Four versions of the Lola T-70. The Aurora 1/32 scale model kit and A-Jet (3259) on the left used the same body shell as the K&B kit (1833). K&B also released the T-70 in 1/24 scale as a kit (1805) and as the body-only shown here (1805-1).

Dan Gurney carried the emblem of K&B Aurora into battle at Riverside, California, on his McLaren Mark 2.

Aurora built the new motor in West Hempstead.

The Challenger was different from the can motors installed in most competitive cars. It had the advantage of being easy to work on and, because it was a sidewinder, placed weight directly over the rear wheels for better traction. Biggest criticism: the Challenger could not match the power of other motors.

Brand realized this from the beginning, so Aurora brought out an improved version—the Super Challenger (1504)—early in 1966. The performance gap was closed when Aurora rewound the Challenger's armatures to transform the 12-volt original into a hot 6-volt power plant.

The K&B connection

A-Jets weren't Aurora's first foray into large-scale slot cars. Through its California subsidiary K&B, Aurora in 1963 marketed 1/25 and 1/24 accessories from a variety of suppliers under the "Model Rama" trademark.

Since K&B served the serious hobbyist market, it was compelled to enter the burgeoning "hot motor" field. K&B's first motor, the Bobcat (1501), debuted early in 1965. A large 36D-size can motor, it was manufactured by can-motor giant Mabuchi of Japan. K&B simply jumped on a well-established bandwagon with the Bobcat; most competitors already sold Mabuchi-built motors.

Mabuchi is one of the great success stories of the hobby industry. Founded after World War II by the Mabuchi brothers, Kenichi and Takaichi, Mabuchi was "discovered" by the Polk brothers in the 1950s building motors in a Tokyo shop with a staff of five women. With U.S. distribution handled by the Polks, Mabuchi achieved tremendous success at a time when Americans had negative images of Japanese-made products. By 1965, Mabuchi had four Tokyo plants employing 1500 workers who built 250,000 motors daily. K&B had tried selling the Aurora Challenger motor in their first slot car kits, but the Mabuchi-made Bobcat's runaway success sealed the American motor's fate.

Aurora's mass-market angle limited their large-scale releases to more intermediate-sized 1/32 cars. This left K&B free to issue cars in larger scales—a natural step, since K&B already marketed 1/24 and 1/25 scale components. In fact, its first 1/25 scale car, the Dragmaster (308), was little more than a metal chassis with a driver's head on top.

K&B's first real 1/25 scale car kits, the Ford GT and Cobra GT (1800 and 1801), were well-received by slot enthusiasts. Their best

K&B 1/25 and 1/24 kit cars. Back row from the left: Ferrari 250 GTO (1803), Porsche 906 (1802), Cobra (1801), and Ford GT (1800). Front row from the left: Chaparral (1804), Lola (1805), and Ferrari 330 P2 (1806).

feature—molded-in clear windows. Other manufacturers' kits required gluing, usually producing ugly smears. K&B retained Ted Neward's contract molding shop in nearby Pomona to design and manufacture integrated clear parts. Neward's process was ingenious: clear windows were first molded separately, then placed into cavities in the body molds before plastic injection. When the cavities filled with molten plastic, heat fused the clear windows to the opaque bodies.

K&B cars ran on an adjustable aluminum chassis, complete with a spring-loaded pick-up arm and realistic, plastic-spoked "aluminum" wheel inserts. The motor was the Challenger sidewinder. *Model Car Science* (March 1965) declared K&B's product line "different from run-of-the-mill kits." Faint praise indeed.

The major drawback—1/25 scale. Almost every other company had standardized at 1/24, but K&B had inherited 1/25 from parent Aurora, which used the size for many of its automotive model kits. In fact, the K&B Ford GT used elements from Aurora's model kit. K&B ultimately fell into line, releasing future cars in 1/24.

K&B issued its first pair of 1/24 cars during the summer of 1965, and praise from slot hobbyists was immediate. The Porsche 906/916 and Ferrari 250 GTO (1802 and 1803) were noted for detailed, lightweight plastic bodies. The Porsche 906 caught some car buffs by surprise; though familiar with the 904, many didn't know Porsche had revamped the car. As it turns out, K&B had received design help on its model directly from Porsche.

The new kits incorporated K&B's latest innovation: the patented Posi-Lok wheel attachment system. Most wheels slipped onto coarsely threaded axles and locked into place with nuts. This usually meant wheels were off-center, sometimes working loose during races. Posi-Lok was simple: wheels stayed in place with a collet—a tapered sleeve you could position anywhere on a smooth axle. Turn a nut, lock the collet, true the wheel position, and your car's tires were locked. For serious racers, this new feature provided a competitive advantage on the racetrack.

Like its corporate parent, K&B moved into ready-to-race 1/24 cars, aimed at serious hobbyists. The new products had Posi-Lok wheels and were powered by various K&B Mabuchi motors. Taking another lesson from Aurora, K&B went against convention and mounted its motors sidewinder-style. And because of K&B's slow release schedule, most cars had the prevailing Mabuchi or Aurora motor of the day.

The first in the series, the Ford Lotus 30 Charger (1850), came with the new 9-volt Royal Bobcat (1500). The Cooper F-1 (1851) of early 1966 was powered by a K&B Wildcat (1505). The Cooper was a narrow-bodied, open-wheel Formula I racer, so it took a smaller 16D-size motor mounted in-line. *Model Car Science* tested the 9-volt Wildcat against the Aurora-built 6-volt Super Challenger in May 1966 and found the

K&B's first two 1/24 cars, the Ferrari 250 GTO and Porsche 906/916

Challenger had better top-end speed on a long track, while the Wildcat performed better on a short, tight track. In a bow to advanced racers' concerns, K&B converted to vacu-formed bodies. The reason: cars with injection-molded bodies looked better, but their heavier weight made them too slow for serious racing.

By 1966 slot car sales had increased so much that K&B expanded to two assembly lines running 16 hours a day. Ten thousand cars rolled off these lines daily. Would it ever end?

Trouble with the licensor

Back in West Hempstead, Aurora's move into large-scale cars led to legal questions involving Aurora's license agreement with Carl Robinette. As intellectual property owner of the basic Aurora HO system, Robinette had been paid royalties on every Model Motoring product made since 1960.

However, when Aurora launched its large-scale slot systems, Robinette asked to be paid the same royalty on the new products. Joe Giammarino offered to pay a smaller fee (1 to 1.5 percent). Robinette refused and filed suit. The case ultimately went to trial, turning on the question of exactly what Robinette had licensed to Aurora. Robinette claimed to have developed the slot car concept.

To investigate Robinette's claims, the court visited a local raceway and watched cars in action. Nat Polk testified on Aurora's behalf—even bringing a 1912 Lionel racing set into the courtroom—to demonstrate that the basic electric car idea was a very old one. Even more compelling was the revelation that unknown to Derek Brand, Robinette had patented the vibrator motor in his own name. Carl Robinette lost the suit, and Aurora paid him in excess of $1 million to buy out his licensor status. Aurora was free from license payments forever.

The peak

1966 was the peak of the slot car boom. *Craft, Model and Hobby Industry* estimated that the United States had more slot raceways than bowling alleys—"over 5,000." More conservative estimates placed the number of properly equipped, full-time race centers at 600. But the dollar figures didn't exaggerate a thing: total sales of slot car equipment had risen from $100 million in 1964 to $170 in 1965, and the growth curve was still headed toward the sky.

As slot fever soared, voices of concern rose. Aurora's regional survey found that in the East "slot centers are popping up like mad," while in California—where the craze had begun—the number was declining. "The quick-rise 'boom days' are nearing an end," Rich Palmer wrote in an August report. "Boom days for these centers lasted from six months to two years and then they began to disappear as fast as they opened up."

There were more insidious problems with large-scale slot cars. Raceways existed for the excitement of competition, but by 1966, a handful of racers in each market had refined their skills so well they won every race. A huge gap developed between most racers and a small group of pros. When average racers discovered they had no hope of winning, they dropped out of the sport for good.

The incessant demand for more speed led to a mad scramble among large-scale slot car manufacturers. Better motors, tires, chassis, and every other racing-car part that might slice a fraction of a second off lap times was marketed. The result was proliferation of new products and rapid obsolescence of the old. Retailers found themselves

Thunderbike (1387), Ford XL500 (1386), Chevy Camaro (1388), and Mercury Cougar (1389)

bombarded with customer demands for the latest products while shelves were still filled with last month's hot items.

Worse, the typical teenage slot racer discovered that building a competitive race car was a very big drain on his allowance. Distributors and retailers were making less money because the numbers of people renting lanes were shrinking and they were regularly stuck with obsolete merchandise they couldn't move. And no one seemed to have the answer.

Aurora's wrong turn, K&B's marginal success

In this hothouse atmosphere, Aurora vowed it would become the leader in 1/32, just as it was in 1/87. The company paid little attention to the warning signs in large-scale slot car racing and forged ahead with grand development plans. And ultimately, it would pay a heavy price.

In 1967 Aurora brought out the innovative slot cycle, the Thundercycle (3266). Unfortunately, in the dwindling large-scale marketing environment, Aurora had chosen the wrong scale in its big-slot gamble. By the mid-1960s most serious slot racers focused on 1/24. MINRA—originally Aurora's clandestine hobby-management organization—found at its 1966 National Drag Championship that 1/24 scale cars outnumbered 1/32 by a margin of six to one. MINRA dropped 1/32 from its 1967 program. To sound the death knell, Aurora 1/32 A-Jets were a commercial failure in department stores.

To further confuse Aurora's perception of large-scale slot cars, its subsidiary K&B continued to enjoy moderate success in large-scale slots. For example, K&B stole the show at HIAA 1966 with its patented Cortina Mechanical Brake. Jose Rodriguez, Jr., reported to *Car Model* (April 1966), "This Cortina mechanical brake by K&B stops like nothing I have ever seen. . . . this was the only real innovation I saw at the show."

Traditional "brake" systems were nothing more than electrical cutoffs. The Cortina, however, was a tiny, lightweight disk brake featuring a central "drum" flanked by two Teflon disks. It fit around a car's rear axle next to the spur gear. On powered track, the brake stayed in the open position and had no effect on the car's performance. However, when current was shut off, the disks clamped together and locked up the rear axle.

With a Cortina brake in his car, a racer—particularly one with a

K&B and Aurora cycles. From the left are Green Machine (3357), Chopper Chariot (3358), and Thundercycle (3266).

The Batmobile in large scale, courtesy K&B (1878).

heavy car—could retain his straightaway speed far more deeply into the curve before having to hit the brake. Suddenly skidding became a real factor in slot car racing, and it took time to master the brake. The Cortina was first sold separately as an accessory, but soon select K&B cars featured it as standard equipment.

The Blue Monster

In the race for more power, Aurora fired another salvo. Critics in the dedicated hobbyist market proclaimed Aurora Challenger motors weren't up to current performance standards. Aurora's answer—the Blue Monster. It was an attempt to free Aurora and K&B from dependence on Mabuchi. Brand later admitted, "We would probably have been better off to buy a Mabuchi, but we were stubborn."

The Blue Monster was another Brand creation, the final evolutionary development of the pancake motor. In this incarnation, the motor's appearance was radically transformed. It was shaped like a conventional can motor, with circular magnets like the Mabuchis. But instead of being fitted into a can, the Blue Monster's magnets were bound together with two metal clips. In essence, the Blue Monster was a very hot 3-volt motor that could turn 50,000 rpms. How would the hobby respond?

Aurora manufactured the Blue Monster in West Hempstead. K&B received a more sedate 12-volt edition called "Hellcat" (1510). K&B marketers hyped the motor's introduction with a "Blue Monster Bonanza" in-store racing contest during the summer of 1966. Their Blue Monster (1895) ready-to-race car was advertised as one that would beat everything on wheels right out of the box. Winners would receive "K&B/Aurora Test Driver" T-shirts and be sent advance copies of new Aurora products.

When the car arrived at retail, hobbyists were pleasantly surprised to find Aurora's Blue Monster car a realistic McLaren I. It ran very well right out of the box, but was not a world-beater. No matter how hard they tried, Aurora marketers simply could not find the silver bullet for success in large-scale slot car racing.

The sure hit

K&B, on the other hand, introduced its "star" product of 1966, the Batmobile (1878), automotive star of the popular ABC television series and a runaway best-selling static model kit and HO slot car for Aurora. K&B made it as a ready-to-run 1/24 scale car with lots of special features: a vacuformed body on aluminum chassis with Cortina brake, Hellcat motor, red pinstriping, lots of chrome, and a blinking

The HO Batmobile and Black Beauty cars, with preproduction test shots in alternate colors

red light on top. At $14.95 it was K&B's most expensive car.

Unfortunately, it did not sell. K&B president John Brodbeck admitted it was a poor racer—evidently not a major concern for K&B during the Batmobile's development.

If the Batmobile had been a success, K&B was prepared to market the Green Hornet's Black Beauty, another TV-inspired product. Aurora's K&B manager Shellie Ostrowe obtained a license agreement from 20th Century Fox, derived in part from the agreement that enabled Aurora to produce a Black Beauty model kit.

In an odd historical footnote, Greenway Productions, producer of *Green Hornet,* used a Black Beauty scale model during special effects sequences that was a 21" pinewood creation of Derek Brand, Andrew Yanchus, and Vic Kowalski. Aurora, it seems, was everywhere in the 1960s—even behind the scenes in Hollywood.

The PRO experience

Despite the serious efforts by MINRA and Aurora to establish industry standards for hobbyist slot car racing, by 1966 there was still no agreement. Aurora's 1960s timeline shows repeated attempts to lead the discussion on standards, beginning with MINRA, but that organization ultimately had proven unsuccessful in bringing local and regional organizations together.

Aurora tried again with PRO—Model Car Racing Professional Organization. West Hempstead distributed blazer patches, window stickers, and organization literature to raceway operators and hobby dealers to bring dealers together in a national organization. There was little response.

Aurora made one last try at a national organization during the 1967 HIAA national convention. HIAA designated MINRA its national organization and set up a committee of industry leaders to lend support. But it was too late; slot racing popularity was already sliding rapidly. When Aurora withdrew advertising from MINRA's *In the Groove* in 1967, the organization folded. However noble the goal, serious slot car racing had proven too meteoric in its rise—and fall—to support a national organization.

Death of a craze

As fast as it had arisen, the slot car boom died. Its faddish character had been obvious from the start, and by 1967 the novelty had worn off. Kids tried slot cars and found them boring, too difficult to master, or too expensive.

Death came quickly for the larger members of the slot car family. The first to go were manufacturers of large-scale slot cars and commercial slot car raceways. Interestingly, the HO segment of slot car manufacture escaped an untimely death; it was less expensive and the average kid could enjoy racing with friends at home. Public raceways by 1967 were sparsely populated by hardcore aficionados hanging on to the bitter end. Never did they represent volume purchasing for firms like Aurora or even K&B.

Overnight Aurora found itself stuck with a large, empty raceway in West Hempstead, Long Island. Silverstein declared it "a very expensive white elephant." Aurora put it on the market, but no buyer could be found. It was ultimately closed at an enormous loss. K&B, the Aurora subsidiary that managed to achieve moderate success in large scale, exited the slot car business in the summer of 1967.

Actually, the collapse was never complete—and commercial raceways never completely disappeared. From the heady days of 1966 when "5000 tracks" were operating, the number declined to about 1500 and stabilized. A cottage industry has continued to produce motors and accessories for die-hard, big-scale slot enthusiasts to this day. Major manufacturers, however, have never returned to the world of large-scale slot cars, and to the general public, the crash of slot cars is defined by the painful year of 1967.

4

TRIALS
amid triumphs

In July 1966 Aurora marked a corporate milestone when it joined the New York Stock Exchange. Abe Shikes, Joe Giammarino, and John Cuomo went on the trading floor with Exchange President Keith Funston to have a photograph taken holding a small Model Motoring layout.

No one enjoyed Aurora's success more than Shikes. He was an extrovert who loved to talk about his business. He once met General Motors chairman Alfred P. Sloan in a Manhattan restaurant and announced: "Last year my firm made more cars than GM!" Then he pulled out a tiny T-jet that he always carried in his pocket and proudly showed it to Sloan.

The best evidence of Aurora's slot car success was its new three-story, 148,000-square-foot facility devoted to HO Model Motoring manufacturing. It was around the corner from the old plant at 44 Cherry Valley Rd. Although operations in the plant were year-round, around the clock, there was a predictable cycle to production. In late December the annual catalog was published, depicting products Aurora intended to market in the upcoming year. Prototypes would be shown to distributors and retailers at the HIAA show in Chicago in late January and at Toy Fair in New York in February. Orders would start to come in, and tooling would be made.

This Penneys set is typical of Aurora's premium packaging: nondescript and easily personalized.

Customized sets and the factory environment

As Model Motoring became the standard in the industry, "private label" sets became an increasingly profitable form of business for Aurora. Specially packaged Model Motoring sets were ordered annually in April by chain-store buyers. Sears, Montgomery Ward, and J. C. Penney were the biggest customers, but Aurora built sets for nearly fifty different retailers. Concepting the sets involved members of sales, R&D, and production managers. Everyone put pencil to paper and designed sets that packed as much value as possible within price ranges set by stores.

Summer and early fall brought a flurry of activity to West Hempstead. Boxes from packaging suppliers came in one door, were placed on the first of six assembly-line conveyor belts, and were progressively filled with track, power packs, controllers, accessories, and cars. When they reached the other end of the plant, they were boxed in cartons and placed on delivery trucks.

Quality Control kept watch over cars as they came off the line. Each Model Motoring car had to make a short run on a section of electrified track. Those that couldn't or ran too slowly were sent back for rework. Cars with average performance went into sets, and those that performed above average were individually boxed and distributed to hobby shops.

The idea was to place the hottest cars into the hobby shops where slot car enthusiasts would see them, buy them, and race them, enhancing Aurora's image as off-the-shelf speed leader.

On the right, America's top GT racers: the Ford GT (1374), Cobra GT (1375), Ford J (1382), and Chevrolet Chaparral (1377). On the track, the foreign competition: a blue Lola GT (1378) and white Porsche 906 (1376). On the left: Chevrolet Mako Shark (1380), Ford Thunderbird (1383), Dino Ferrari (1381), and Olds Toronado (1379).

Shipping was full tilt from August to December. New York retailers' trucks were still backing up to the loading dock on December 24th. January to March was another surge period, restocking the rest of the country. Then HIAA and Toy Fair, and the whole process would begin again. It was a cycle that rang cash registers across the country and filled Aurora's accounts.

What to do with the Grand National?

By 1966 the novelty had worn off the Ford-Aurora Grand National, and Aurora had to work hard to get hobby shops to participate. Aurora pledged merchandise prizes to the three shops showing the most enterprise in promoting the program, even if their stores didn't produce a state winner. Stores also received special metallic-plated Ford Thunderbirds and XL 500s (1383, 1386) that were premiums for taking part.

The Fifth Grand National began in the fall as Ford unveiled its new 1967 models. Aurora was given advance drawings of the 1967 Thunderbird and XL 500 to develop slot cars. Symbolic of the Grand National's decline was the fact that the final was televised only on local New York kid show *Wonderama*. The winner: 14-year-old Rick Hanna of Galesburg, Illinois.

Silverstein's greatest Grand National disappointment was ABC's repeated refusal to cover the annual championships on *Wide World of Sports*. As the network repeatedly told him, they did not consider slot car racing a real sport.

You can't fool kids: Cigarbox

When 1967 arrived, the mature Model Motoring line had a new challenge to face—the explosive debut of Mattel Hot Wheels. Miniature die-casts had been around since the Tootsietoys of the 1920s, and Matchbox had become world leader in the 1950s. But Hot Wheels and their truly innovative frictionless axles changed the die-cast game forever, and slot cars began to feel the heat.

Never timid to join a fight, Aurora jumped in head first. Anson Isaacson, recently hired away from Ideal Toys to advise Aurora's new games and toys division, believed

American children knew repackaged slot cars when they saw them. And talk about derivative packaging—can you say "Matchbox"?

Aurora could become a leader in die-cast. Isaacson, Silverstein, and Schwarzchild rented a hotel room away from the bustle of West Hempstead and brainstormed. When they emerged from their seclusion, they had come up with "Cigarbox Cars," autos individually packaged in miniature boxes with flip-top lids resembling tiny cigar boxes—clearly a derivative of Matchbox's enduring packaging theme.

Aurora had one distinct advantage: it could market dozens of cars immediately because of their existing slot car tooling. Competitors couldn't develop and produce variety and volume like Aurora. Create a die-cast chassis, install Thunderjet wheels and tires, and combine it with existing Thunderjet bodies—Cigarbox. Aurora delivered its first 26 of a planned 72 cars in January.

Aurora invested a good deal of money to tool Cigarbox. Two lines capable of 30,000 cars daily were established. The only problem—a total and complete lack of demand. After the Arburg machines spewed out two weeks' worth of bodies, Cigar Box manufacture ceased. As Brand observed, kids weren't fooled—Aurora's "die-casts" were simply revamped slot bodies without the glamour of Hot Wheels or cute details of Matchbox. Only two runs of Cigarbox cars were ever produced.

Speedline: low-rent lemonade from expensive lemons

Faced with this disaster, Aurora changed course. Isaacson announced a new line that would rise from the ashes of Cigarbox—Speedline cars and track. This time Aurora took the easy route and copied Mattel.

In creating Speedline, Aurora retained the die-cast Cigarbox chassis. Brand added a new axle and hard-plastic wheels to roll on Aurora's Hot Wheels-derivative orange strip track. Also announced were several jumps, loops, and other track accessories.

Speedline sold very well in 1969; Mattel couldn't keep pace with demand. But as Bill Silverstein traveled the country in 1970, he discovered that youngsters wanted Hot Wheels, not Speedline. Despite his warnings, Aurora continued to manufacture Speedlines—and store them in warehouses. It would take years to sell off the inventory.

Aurora never completely abandoned Speedline. Production resumed at Aurora's Singapore plant. A second edition of Speedline cars

Speedline. Hot Wheels, anyone?

on new yellow-and-orange blister-cards came out in 1973, and a third edition (called Superspeedsters) was released in 1975. They were so cheap that retailers had to mark them down decisively to move them. Once again, straying from its core product line—HO Model Motoring—had proven disastrous for Aurora. And to the detriment of the West Hempstead manufacturer, the straying had only begun.

Changes in the wind

The failed venture into die-cast was part of a larger corporate agenda. Aurora by the late 1960s had adopted a corporate strategy to move into the mainstream of toys and games, a treacherous land where the profit margin potential—and risk—was much greater.

Derek Brand played a part in setting these changes into motion. Already he had drastically altered the course of Aurora Plastics Corporation when he developed HO slot cars. Change came again, this time in 1966, when Brand developed a new game in his Model Motoring lab.

Because of his heritage, Derek Brand was fond of the old English pub game skittles. In it, players knocked down wooden pins on a small platform by swinging a ball tethered to a pole anchored in the game base. Brand created a prototype and showed it first to Joe Giammarino, then to Abe Shikes and Bill Silverstein.

The concept became Skittle Bowl, a fun, hands-on diversion that would become the best-selling game of 1969 and 1970. Ever wary of opportunity, Shikes believed that Skittle Bowl represented Aurora's "big break" to legitimately expand into toys. Giammarino, on the other hand, thought Skittle Bowl was a "one-in-a-million" lucky hit.

As difficult as it is to believe today, the ensuing disagreement over Skittle Bowl and its ultimate importance in Aurora's future became so profound that the original partnership—Shikes, Cuomo, and Giammarino—would break up. Long-simmering tensions among Aurora's top men had finally boiled over.

The 1967–71 period was a major transitional period for Aurora. In 1967 John Cuomo escaped the harsh front-office atmosphere by retiring. A year later the company's board of directors forced Joe Giammarino to

Charles Diker, the investor who would bring Nabisco into the world of Aurora.

leave the company he had helped found. "I was fired from my own company," he declared.

Then in 1969 a group of investors headed by Charles M. Diker bought a controlling interest in Aurora, prompting Abe Shikes to retire a year later. In 1971 Aurora's new owners sold out to food giant Nabisco. Within three whirlwind years, Aurora Plastics Corporation had become a completely different company. This transformation was symbolized by a new, Nabisco-selected name for the firm: Aurora Products Corporation.

Nabisco president Lee S. Bickmore declared "great potential" for Aurora as the West Hempstead toymaker expanded into games and toys. Nabisco's strategy focused on aggressive, rapid gross-sales growth to establish a dominant market position in games and toys. As the logic went, operating losses would be expected during this growth phase, but once the leadership role had been established, profits would soon follow.

As events unfolded, that's just how the strategy played out—sort of. Gross sales increased rapidly, but Aurora, which had never lost money, began posting sizable deficits each year. Change was not kind to Aurora.

AURORA
BIG CAR RACING
1971

Aurora brought back 1/32 scale cars in 1970–71, but they quickly went out of the picture.

Late-'60s slots: McLaren-Elva (1397), Mangusta Mongoose (1400), Dune Buggy roadster (1398) and coupe (1399). Also factory test shots of a silver-plated Dune Buggy body and McLaren with no paint detailing.

The new visionary

With the investor-led sale to Nabisco and the departure of Abe Shikes, Aurora got a new president: Charles M. Diker, a young, cigar-smoking former vice president of cosmetics giant Revlon. In no uncertain terms, Diker aimed to transform Aurora. No more Shikes-inspired seat-of-the-pants planning. Aurora would change from a hobby-oriented firm to a games-oriented toymaker.

Accompanying Diker's new vision was a major personnel shake-up. Many longtime Aurora department heads either departed or were fired. With the new emphasis on games and toys, neglect pervaded Aurora's original product line, plastic model kits. Model Motoring continued to receive strong—even increased—support. Diker felt that slot cars had growth potential in the toy market.

Brand not only survived the bloodletting, but actually benefited. He was promoted to Vice President for Research and Development, and in 1970 introduced a product illustrating Aurora's new emphasis on toys. "Powerslicks" had been devised by Fred Addicks of Innova, a California design company. He showed it to Brand, who brought the system into production. Powerslicks' major feature: straight track sections were powered, while the remainder was flexible enough to mold into banked curves.

When Powerslicks 1/32 scale cars hit the powered strips, kids pushed power buttons and the cars' momentum was greatly enhanced. Power came from six D-cell batteries. Sets featured black power sections and bright orange and lavender curves. The first two cars were mod-customized "thingies" created by HMS. Later Innova added four conventional cars to the line. Unfortunately, the toy's concept was flawed: car pickup shoes dragged during the gliding phase, causing the cars to stop before they reached the powered straights. Powerslicks lasted two years.

State of the union: Model Motoring

Sales of Aurora's mainline Thunderjet HO sets continued to increase in the late 1960s, even though the initial burst of enthusiasm had long since passed. HO sales hadn't been hurt by the collapse of large scale slots. Indeed, the big-slot crash probably helped Thunderjets, since it caused Aurora to channel most

Evolving Model Motoring packaging, from the jewel box of the Willys Gasser (1401, foreground) to the Tuff Ones' plinth-based tower

remaining slot car funding into HO.

As the 1960s drew to a close, Aurora began to make real improvements in Model Motoring. Perhaps most important from an operating standpoint was the evolution of the speed controller.

From the earliest days, Aurora's novel steering-wheel controller had been criticized as cute but clumsy. In 1965 it had been abandoned for a plunger-type controller with a thumb button (1347). This design was unique because it worked by compressing a stack of silicon wafers inside the plunger. It improved electrical flow through the controller—and thus increased speed. Unfortunately, the new design generated too much heat, a problem for any handheld device. As a correction, Aurora introduced the Mark II controller (1346) in 1969, but poor design caused its internal parts to stick.

To solve this problem, Aurora hired Jim Russell, large-scale slot car industry veteran and K&B consultant. Russell was glad to join Aurora; with the crash of large-scale slots, "my business had deteriorated to virtually nothing."

Russell's controller (1345) was based on a product his old company had marketed. Its pistol shape was innovative, and in 1969 Aurora began including it in sets. The controller put the resistor—and its heat—into the pistol's "barrel." It also changed actuation from thumb movement to a more sensitive finger trigger. The design was a

Dodge Chargers in various states of decoration and assembly (1407), along with the 1408 Ford Torino. The all-green bodies are factory test shots.

Alfa Romeo Type 33 (1409) with and without chrome details, Chaparral 2F (1410), Pontiac GTO in two desirable color schemes (1411), AMX (1414), and Mustang Mach I (1415). Also, three factory prototype bodies that never reached store shelves.

permanent solution to Aurora's controller problems.

But Russell was hired for more than just his controller. Charles Diker wanted someone with serious experience in large-scale slot cars to help Aurora revive the 1/32 slot car segment. Aurora's president believed the larger A-jets would be more appropriate as Christmas gifts. Russell believed Diker's attempted revival was a losing proposition, but he agreed to support the project—"to my undying shame," he later confessed.

To accompany the A-jet relaunch, development progressed on an all-new inexpensive track system. As a scaled-up copy of HO track, the new A-jet track had power rails set away from the slot. The result of this costly retooling debuted in Aurora's 1970–71 Big Car Racing catalogs—but the concept never sold. "Performance was nonexistent," observed Russell. "To say the least, it was a total flop." For the record, the new A-jet set contained a Ferrari 612 and McLaren M12 (3351, 3352) and a Mirage Coupe and Ferrari 312P (3353, 3354), but only two chassis for the four bodies. In 1971 a set of "Crazy California" wheelie-trikes (3357, 3358) were added to the 1/32 line, mainly to use up existing inventory before shutting down the line.

Back in the world of HO . . .

During this time Aurora continued with its Model Motoring upgrade program. In 1969 Aurora introduced an HO car that was a clear improvement on the six-year-old Thunderjet design. Aurora called the new cars "Wild Ones": a Mustang, Ford GT, Camaro, and Cougar (1416 through 1419). Though the bodies were regular T-jets, they were molded in snow-white plastic, striped, numbered, and decorated with company logos like STP and Pennzoil.

More changes awaited under the hood. Aurora designers stuffed a T-jet motor with hotter wound armatures, a new gear ratio, silver-plated pickups and brushes for improved conductivity, and soft sponge rubber tires. The cars were indeed "the fastest cars ever made," as the ads said, but real increases in speed were marginal.

Perhaps Aurora developed Wild Ones because it sensed a looming war with its one remaining HO

Wild Ones packaging features this stunning Camaro art.

competitor, Tyco. The New Jersey-based train and slot car manufacturer had been making inexpensive sets for the Christmas market throughout the 1960s, but Aurora dominated both mass and hobbyist sales. Tyco was perennially left with whatever remained.

In 1968, however, Tyco made news when it improved the quality of its car bodies. Hobbyists noted the changes and began speculating that Tyco was preparing for a serious run at Aurora. That speculation proved prophetic in 1970 with the launch of TycoPros. Promoted with a strong hobby advertising campaign, TycoPros featured an inexpensive Mabuchi HT-50 in-line can motor crammed into a wide, low-slung pan chassis. The design allowed the motor to efficiently transmit power to the rear axle through a simple two-gear linkage. With wide racing slicks to grip the track, TycoPros were the fastest out-of-the-box cars available—except when they broke down, which was frequently.

The arrival of TycoPros threw West Hempstead's R&D staff into pandemonium. "Everybody was having a stroke," recalled Derek Brand. He considered the T-jet a better product for the home market. After all, its rugged construction represented a clear advantage to a toy manufacturer. However, when it came to the needs of serious slot car

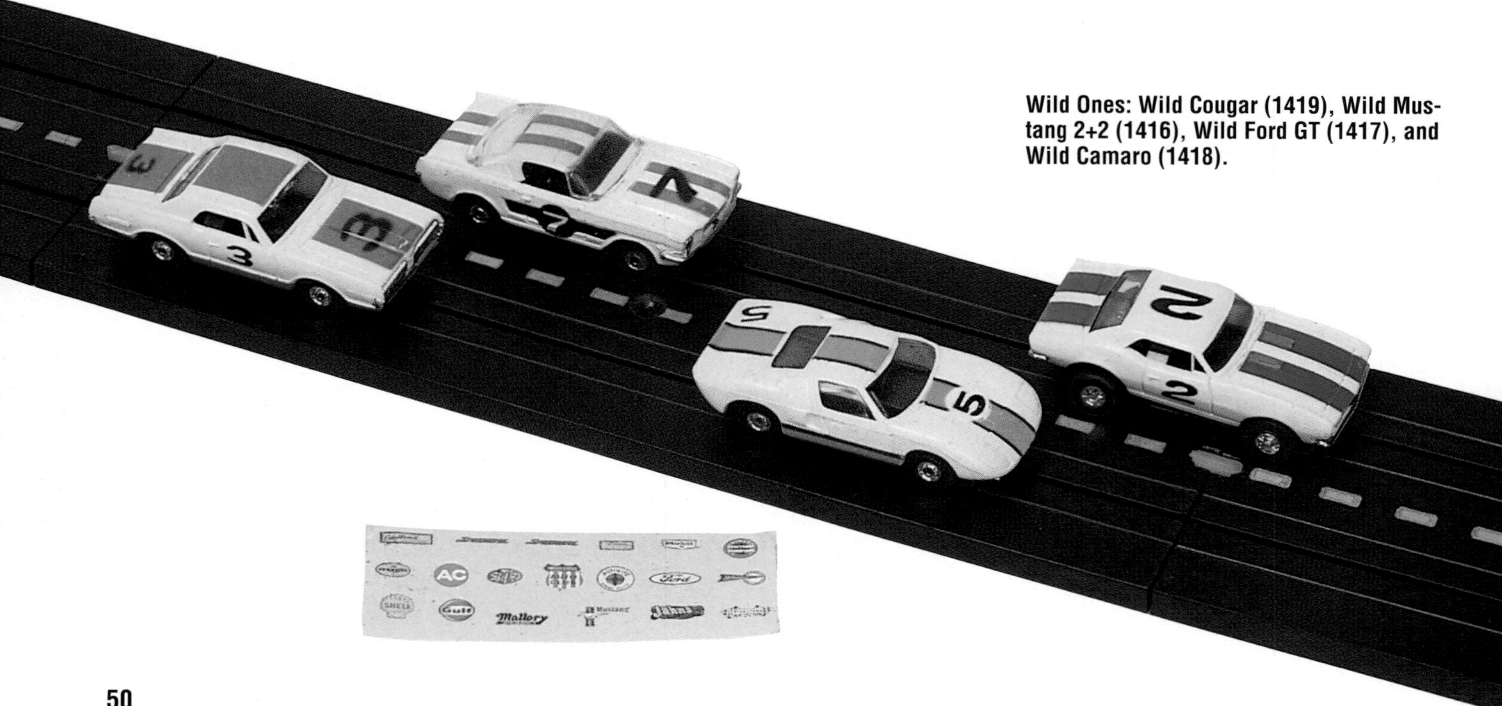

Wild Ones: Wild Cougar (1419), Wild Mustang 2+2 (1416), Wild Ford GT (1417), and Wild Camaro (1418).

Lemon and yellow Flower Power Volkswagens (1404), Cheetah (1403), Firebird (1402), Formula 1 Repco Brabham (1406), Formula 1 McLaren BRM (1405).

'32 Ford pickup (1421), Flamethrower McLaren Elva (1431), Flamethrower Ford J (1430), and a variety of Chevy El Caminos (1429). Also factory tests with nonproduction plastic colors.

Above: The Tuff Ones. Dino Ferrari (1481), Ford GT (1472), Dune Buggy coupe (1473), Cheetah (1475), Willys Gasser (1474), Chaparral 2F (1476).

Below: On left, the three production versions of the #5 Tuff Ones AMX (1477). Yellow firebird (1478) and test shot red body are at top. Also shown: #21 Cougar (1479), #1 production Camaro (1480), and three prototype #4 bodies. Production Lola GT (1471) and Volkswagen (1482) with prototype bodies are at top.

Tuff Ones inspired all sorts of creative marketing, including "giveaways" of straight track sections.

hobbyists, Brand had to admit the Tyco cars were indeed faster.

It wasn't long before Aurora's reply arrived: Tuff Ones. Part of Jim Russell's new role within Aurora was to act as the firm's "expert" spokesman to the slot car fraternity. As a result, he was a natural for introducing Tuff Ones in December 1969. Russell emphasized the Tuff Ones' new "radially oriented" magnets, which made the Thunderjet motor run faster with less heat. Tuff Ones' new soft sponge-rubber tires would "dig in" on curves. Most important, Aurora would promote the cars with ads on Saturday morning kids' TV, CBS's *Lassie*—and to hit adults who did the buying, *Championship Bowling*.

As icons of their time, Tuff Ones looked flashier than any previous Model Motoring product. Bright yellow, bright white, orange, pink, and lime green—such was the domain for slot cars. This was 1970, after all.

Of course, serious slot racers were more concerned with performance. *Car Model* ran articles on the Tuff Ones. Dale Flanagan (May 1970) judged them "sort of a 'Wild One' with hormone shots. . . . more evolutionary than revolutionary." Tom Malone (December 1970) found TycoPros faster and Tuff Ones quicker on braking. This suggested that Tycos would be better on large tracks and Auroras on small, tight ones. Ed Bianchi (February 1971) thought Tuff Ones brought some long-needed improvements to the T-jet motor, but his speed tests showed "an awesome gap in performance. . . . the TycoPro made mince-meat of the Tuff One in all departments." Like Malone, he thought Aurora braking power might even the competition on a real track.

Selling the Tuff Ones

Tyco or no Tyco—when it came to slot car marketing, no one could compare to Aurora. Bill Silverstein pulled out all the stops for Tuff Ones. Aurora's new cars starred in the most extravagant slot car production ever staged for television in November 1970. Silverstein had tried for years to get Aurora on Ed Sullivan's popular Sunday night TV variety show. He finally sold Sullivan on the idea of a $50,000 match race between the world's top Grand Prix drivers. CBS thought Silverstein was crazy to spend $50,000 on a toy car race, but Silverstein saw it another way—he received seven minutes of prime time for his money during a time when one minute cost $80,000. (There was, of course, a stiff price: Aurora's name was never mentioned during the segment.)

On the eve of the Sullivan show, Aurora's Dick Schwarzchild presided over a dinner at Sardi's Restaurant in Manhattan. Four champion drivers were on hand: America's clean-cut Dan Gurney and Great Britain's heavily sideburned trio of Graham Hill, Stirling Moss, and Jackie Stewart. Each honed his slot car driving skills by racing with Aurora's R&D staff. ("How many people can say they've raced against Jackie Stewart?" gushed one Aurora employee.) At the dinner Aurora's track played host to races between the stars and newsmen covering the event. Jackie Stewart: "I think children can do it better than we can!"

Aurora's real-life racers plying the slotted track: Dan Gurney, Graham Hill, Stirling Moss, and Jackie Stewart. The Scotsman won the $50,000 grand prize. Sportscaster Bill Mazer calls the race.

Aurora on the *Ed Sullivan Show,* if in spirit only—Sullivan refused to allow Aurora's name to be mentioned.

At Saturday morning's *Ed Sullivan Theater* rehearsal, Stewart's quip proved true (at least for a few seconds) as all four drivers wiped out on the first curve. During the evening's live broadcast it was Sullivan's turn to goof up, mispronouncing just about everyone's name.

The race, thankfully, was very exciting. Aurora's 32-foot track featured prototypes of the new banked curves. Each led at some point during the 20-lap race, but in the end Stewart prevailed over Gurney and won the $35,000 top prize. In perminute terms, it was the richest purse ever offered in a Grand Prix-style race.

5

A/FX
a new era

A transition set, still lacking the A/FX branding but featuring A/FX car artwork

During the summer of 1970, Derek Brand—survivor of the Nabisco takeover—quit Aurora. He felt cramped by Nabisco's management style—"too many meetings"—and returned to California, where he and his son started their own toy design house.

Brand's successor as Vice President for Research and Development was Walter Moe, an Ideal Toys veteran who had worked for Aurora since 1968. Nabisco was demanding that Aurora's gross sales increase drastically, and they gave Moe sufficient resources to fund development. During Aurora's original partnership era, R&D had been a barebones operation. Moe quickly added equipment and staff to create a genuine research facility.

Born in Germany, Walter Moe spoke with a strong accent and willingly accepted the role of Prussian drillmaster. He saw his job as one of recruiting young men—"talented, spirited fellows"—and demanding results. "I didn't try to win popularity contests," he later declared, though he believed in rewarding creative people for achievement.

Moe described Nabisco's management philosophy as one in which various midlevel executives were thrown "into the gladiators' ring, where only the strong would survive." Departmental jurisdictions overlapped, an unavoidable reality, since R&D, Engineering, Marketing, and Sales all collaborated to get a product on the shelves. Product managers (such as the head of slot cars) were several steps down the chain of command, with "lots of responsibilities and very little authority." However, product managers (with R&D under them) developed new concepts, which they pitched to the men up the corporate ladder for decisions. This upward flow of innovation drove the product line—and the corporation.

Rethinking slot cars

When Derek Brand departed, Charles Diker transferred Model Motoring leadership to Jim Keeler, the recently hired product manager of Aurora model kits. For a while he ran both lines—with two sets of headaches. Although only 30, Keeler was a well-known figure in the hobby industry; he'd helped produce Revell Rat Fink hot rod figure kits in the early 1960s. Slender with dark-rimmed glasses, Keeler looked the part of a model fanatic.

Jim Keeler was given a single job: develop a new car that would beat TycoPros yet still sell as an inexpensive mass-market toy. At the very least, Aurora needed to narrow the performance gap. This meant a car with better speed, improved handling, and enhanced body detail—not to mention easy

This new ad appeared in model magazines prior to release of the A/FX line to create demand for the product.

The first A/FXs: Super II (1788), Grand Am funny car (1702), Corvette "A" production (1703), Datsun Baja pickup (1745), '29 Ford Model A woody (1746), Porsche 917 Can-Am (1747), Dodge street van (1748), #7 Auto World McLaren XLR (1752), #15 Ferrari Can-Am 612 (1751).

manufacture, rugged-build quality, and low price.

The new car needed a new name. Wild Ones and Tuff Ones were out of the question, and other suggestions—including Wipe-Outs, Muscle Machines, Street Cleaners, Super Cars, or Boss Machines—just didn't cut it. After an all-day brainstorming session, Keeler had his name: A/FX, derived from National Hot Rod Association classification terms—A (hot stock sports cars) and FX for factory experimental.

Model Motoring would not die so easily, however. As one of the few remaining old-timers, Dick Schwarzchild argued that Aurora had too much invested in "Model Motoring" to give it up. Jim Russell also strongly opposed the name change. "I blew my stack," he later recalled. "I thought it was stupid to associate our line with the dirty T-shirt-and-leather jacket guys."

But Diker liked the new name, so A/FX was in. As a partial compromise, "Model Motoring" continued in small letters under A/FX. The slash in A/FX would disappear in 1973.

Innovation—sort of

When A/FX cars reached stores in 1971, experts raised their eyebrows. The heart of the car was still the same old pancake motor. However, evolutionary changes did exist—and they made a difference. The most visible modification was the chassis. In his last contribution before leaving Aurora, Derek Brand and chief machinist Victor Kowalski added vent holes to aid motor cooling. In addition, new axle positioning lowered the car.

Tires were wider and softer. A new blade slot guide (as opposed to the basic pin) improved the car's track hold. A/FX bodies snapped onto chassis "ears," making it easy to access the motor and gears.

The A/FX bodies represented Aurora's best work. Improvements in detail were Moe's and Keeler's response to Tyco's popular new car

The wide variety of A/FX packaging, from Super II to late Magna-Traction

styling. Keeler: "Tyco had been making tremendous inroads with K-Mart and Sears. Their individual cars were doing extremely well." As a modeler, Keeler was accustomed to intricate detail on 1/24 scale static models. He saw no reason why 1/80 scale cars couldn't be better. In its search for better styling, Aurora ended its long relationship with HMS.

The new design team

With no fallback position in the form of HMS, Aurora took design completely in-house. The new patternmaker was Ron Klein, a young man from California recommended by Jim Russell. Klein was an independent stylist who worked from his own design drawings. He had sculpted the earlier Russkit cars. Klein's sculpting style was described as "cartoonish," but it looked good in HO scale—perhaps more realistic than a truly accurate rendition. Klein loved European sports cars and wanted Aurora to make lots of them.

This sometimes led to clashes with Keeler, who revered American street machines. The debate's legacy was a creative mix of car designs, executed in the best detail ever offered in HO.

Klein was entrusted by Keeler with Aurora sports car design, but Keeler went to the prestigious Art Center in Los Angeles to hire a designer for the rest of the line. Richard "Rake" Ratkiewich had hoped to go to Detroit, like many Art Center grads, but instead went to West Hempstead. Rake later raided his alma mater for more talent. John Vernon showed that he had mastered the toy company technique of designing models from magazine photos; he became Ratkiewich's number two. In 1973, Art Center alum Ken Hill joined the company. Ratkiewich, Vernon, and Hill became the A/FX design department for all Detroit-inspired cars. (Never slow for work, the three also styled Aurora toys and games.)

The difficulties of design

Chief among challenges for slot car designers was the fact that bodies had to be distorted in order to fit over motors and onto standard chassis with fixed wheelbases. To make matters worse, autos differing in size—from a NASCAR stocker to a Volkswagen—had to ride the same slot car chassis. Ratkiewich made the strategic decision to design each car to fit its wheelbase, rather than match scale among A/FX cars. A NASCAR racer would thus be smaller than a Volkswagen.

Wheels posed another dilemma. Ones that rolled well were invariably too big for the car's overall scaling, creating huge wheel wells in the tiny fenders. To the dismay of the designers, there was no simple solution for cars forced to ride on a standard A/FX chassis. A "specialty chassis" with smaller front wheels and oversized rear wheels was introduced and used on some models.

Despite these challenges, the A/FX design team created some of the best-looking slot cars of all time. Mike Meyers paid tribute to his designers' use of "incredibly creative cheating" in making their tiny car models look like the real thing.

Plastic played a big role in innovation as well. A/FX cars began to feature a new variety of plastic colors and paint schemes. "We drove Dow [Chemical] crazy" with requests for exotic plastic colors, Keeler recalled. Ratkiewich's designers created three different color and paint schemes for each car.

The hot-selling 1957 Chevy Nomad (1760) received the widest range of body and tinted window plastic combinations. "We did it in umpity different colors," said Keeler. (Not surprisingly, when Tomy AFX reissued the Nomad 20 years later in 1993, it immediately became the best-selling car in the line!)

The effort to get 1971's A/FX cars into production paralleled the rush to bring out vibrators in 1960. "We worked our tails off seven days a week," remembered Ratkiewich. The effort paid off.

"A/FX sales went through the roof," declared Keeler. "We couldn't make them fast enough." Aurora slot car revenues would triple—from $15 million in 1970 to $45 million in 1976

Internal battles and the rise of Can-Am

A/FX success was actually a vindication of sorts. Aurora marketing executives had argued that money spent on development of a variety of cars would be wasted. Sales, they believed, would be the same if Aurora offered only a few basic car types, track options, and accessories.

Jim Keeler argued that bringing out a continuous flow of new cars made slot racing a year-round hobby, not just a Christmas toy destined for the closet. As long as Junior's track was set up, he'd be buying new cars and accessories—the real profit driver for Aurora. Keeler's argument won the day.

Among the most popular A/FX cars of the period were Aurora's Can-Am road-course racers. Carved by Ron Klein, the models evoked the thrilling vehicles that raced by top drivers across early-1970s America and Canada. Aurora took the headline-making Can-Am concept and shrewdly turned it into a best-selling slot car line. The series debuted with the Ferrari 612 and Auto World McLaren (1751, 1752). Keeler attended the inaugural Can-Am race, took photographs of every car, and had slot versions in production six weeks later—record time for Aurora. Unfortunately, lead time would never be this good again; by the mid-1970s, Aurora would require 18 months to bring a slot car to market.

Aurora's final Can-Am racers were the RC Cola Porsche 917-10K and Porsche/Audi 510K (1747, 1786). Aurora marketers cut a deal with Sears to produce the super-hot Porsche/Audi. Jim Keeler took the first shot of the 510K to Watkins Glenn and showed it to owner Roger Penske and driver Mark Donahue. Keeler was amused when the conversation turned to whether the slot car's tiny movable rear spoiler was functional. "I wish I had a tape recording of that conversation," Keeler recalled. Interestingly, Penske's real-life Porsche proved so dominant on the Can-Am circuit that it may have contributed to the series' 1974 demise.

Emergence of the Orient

With the advent of A/FX, only body design and patternmaking remained at West Hempstead. Everything else—including manufacturing—had been transferred to the Orient. When Aurora engineers finished design work, patterns were air-expressed to the Far East, where molds were cut, bodies were produced, and cars were assembled. Ratkiewich demanded that first painted prototypes be sent to West Hempstead for approval before production began. His reason: Hong Kong and Singapore graphic artists tended to "orientalize" decoration schemes.

Actually, Aurora had begun transferring production to the Orient in 1968, when they purchased 49 percent interest in Johnson Electric of Hong Kong. This firm became Aurora's motor manufacturer, allowing West Hempstead plant managers to free up floor space for toy and game production. Then in the mid-1970s, Aurora moved most production from Hong Kong to Singapore to take advantage of tax breaks. By then the only remaining A/FX manufacture in West Hempstead was packaging.

The Far East wasn't the only region to get Aurora's slot car business. Aurora's subsidiary in Rexdale, Canada, packaged Model Motoring sets, and a plant in Juarez, Mexico, contributed to A/FX production by making controllers and track. The reason for Aurora's diversification was simple: Aurora had to internationalize in order to lower costs and remain competitive. And in doing so, Aurora presaged the 1980s trend of overseas toy manufacture—a trend that today is a fact of American toymaking life.

Thunderjets—end of the line

During the first two years of A/FX, Aurora continued to list some Thunderjets in its catalog. After all, there was a huge T-jet inventory in the Aurora warehouse (Keeler:

Final Thunderjets: the Dune Buggy (1483), Super modified roadster (1484), Snowmobile (1485), and Good Humor premium truck (1487)

Dodge Charger Daytona (1753), Too Much (1754), Turbo Turnon (1755), Trans-Am Camaro Z28 (1756), Porsche 917 (1757), Plymouth Cuda funny car (1758), Vega Van "Gasser" (1759), and Chevy Nomad (1760).

"literally mountains"), and the West Hempstead toymaker had to get rid of it somehow. In fact, a large quantity of leftover T-jet chassis compelled Aurora to design four new Thunderjet bodies for distribution in the toy and novelty market.

The Super Modified Roadster (1484) was only a slight departure from the slot car mainstream. Remarkably, it used the body of the ancient Vibrator Hot Rod (1553, 1365) from the early 1960s. The "Sand Van" Dune Buggy and "Bushwhacker" Snowmobile (1483, 1485) were totally out of bounds. The Sand Vans came in a race set with orange "Baja colored" track; the Snowmobile came with snow-white track. These low-cost sets sold quickly and cleared Aurora's surplus inventory in short order.

The final Thunderjet was also the cutest: Good Humor Ice Cream Truck (1487). Aurora marketing managers cut a deal with Good Humor to produce 5,000 low-priced sets for sale as premiums. Good Humor not only paid tooling costs, they even supplied a real-life truck to copy. The R&D staff drove it around the parking lot at the West Hempstead plant, burning rubber and ringing the bell, all part and parcel of standard model research.

And that was the last of the Thunderjets.

Super II: memoirs of a teen racer

A/FX cars were becoming serious business for racer hobbyists. Not only were they doing well in the mass market, but the survivors of the large-scale slot car crash were adapting their interests to Aurora's innovations in HO. When the first A/FX cars were tested by *Car Model* magazine, staff editors determined that the A/FXs could match or beat TycoPros in every department—except top speed.

The reason: superiority of the can motor over Aurora's pancake design. Of course, the motor made little difference on home tracks where speeds were slow. Most important, the slight TycoPro speed advantage meant nothing to the millions of kids who got Aurora sets for Christmas—and Aurora was still as dominant as ever when it came to mass sales.

Hardcore slot racers—those who were now HO enthusiasts—were a different story. Generally speaking, these hobbyists used can motors like Mabuchis in Tyco cars. With such a motor-chassis combination, it seems obvious that the TycoPros would dominate their Aurora counterparts. And nowhere was this

Ford "Baja Bronco" (1769), Dodge Charger stock car (1773), Bre-Datsun 240Z (1775) and Bre-Datsun 510 Trans-Am (1776), Chevy Bel Air (1777), Volkswagen "Baja Bug" (1778), and two screamers, the Lola T-260 Can-Am (1767) and Shadow Can-Am (1768).

Some examples of the popular Plymouth Road Runner with Richard Petty-inspired "43" (1762), Pinto funny car (1761), Ferrari 512M (1763), AMC Javelin Trans-Am (1764), Javelin pro stocker (1765), Corvette funny car (1766).

more clearly demonstrated than at a summer 1971 race held at Brooklyn's Buzz-A-Rama center. Thirty-two can-motored cars were matched against just two cars with Aurora Thunderjet motors. However, to the amazement of everybody, one of the Aurora-powered cars easily defeated the field.

The winning driver—Brooklyn high school senior Tony Porcelli. One phone call from Buzz-A-Rama to Keeler at West Hempstead, and the Aurora slot car product manager was asking Porcelli to join the Aurora team (as soon as he graduated from school, of course). With Aurora's sponsorship, Porcelli racked up wins on the slot car circuit with his modified A/FX.

Meanwhile, West Hempstead R&D went to work on a new A/FX production car that incorporated Porcelli's innovations. It was intended to be a prestige item showcasing Aurora technology. Marketers planned to introduce the new car at the 1972 HIAA Show as the "Fastest Slot Car in the World." However great a promotional idea it was, Porcelli finished second at the year's final race.

Between races, Porcelli worked at the West Hempstead plant with the R&D team. He recalls how much he enjoyed working with other enthusiasts. Great esprit de corps prevailed among the R&D staff, 18 men who labored in an exciting work atmosphere and proudly wore team blazers and lapel pins.

Outside his department, however, Porcelli found too much dissension and infighting. "We butted heads regularly with engineering and marketing," he recalled. As a result, Porcelli's modified A/FX car "turned out to be a real nightmare. I did all the work on the prototypes—designing them, building them, and racing them—and turned them over to Engineering. R&D was still supposed to work with Engineering, but there was a lot of friction between the two departments." The car based on Porcelli's design differed greatly from the car he had been racing. "I was disappointed. I really was."

The altered Porcelli design debuted at the HIAA convention as the Super II (1788). Car Model's Howard Kilgore ran the prototype at the show, and his reaction was very positive: "Saying the car is a pleasure to drive is an understatement! The sensation of controlling an HO car with blinding speed and superb handling characteristics is pure enjoyment. . . . The car will compare with the very best scratchbuilts when total performance is considered." Aurora slot car chief Jim Keeler labeled it "a holy terror."

The Super II resembled Tony Porcelli's prototype, but changes had been made to accommodate mass production. Lead weights were installed differently. Certain metal components were too soft. Braided copper pickups were terrific for electrical pickup but turned into a matted mess with use. Most disappointing were the rear tires. They were supposed to be wide and soft but were too narrow and too hard—and the motor was just too much for the tires.

The slot car community's chief criticism was the car's price—$12 compared to $4 for a regular A/FX.

The fabulous Toy Fair raceway for 1972. Two levels of action showcased the performance and selection available to buyers of Aurora AFX. Howard Johansen photo.

Peace Tank (1782), Roarin' Rolls "Golden Ghost" (1781), Porsche 510K Can-Am (1786), Matador stock car (1787), Ford Model A panel (1791), Flamethrower Ferrari 512M (1799) and Flamethrower Porsche 917 (1798).

Some wondered if HO racing would price itself out of existence, just as 1/24 cars had. But despite its problems, the Super II kept up with the best scratchbuilts, and kids didn't have to be experts to keep it on track through the curves. Dale Flanagan of *Car Model* (October 1972) concluded, "Whether it's worth the $12 price tag is something you (and your banker) will have to decide." The Super II would last only two years, 1972 and 1973.

High Performance Track

Aurora built its most elaborate slot raceway ever for 1972's New York Toy Fair. Showcasing the Super II was a beautifully landscaped 3 x 16-foot monster of plywood, chicken wire, and plaster. The road course climbed up and around a foot-high mountain while a four-lane speedway oval with banked curves nestled in the valley below.

More than just a showcase for the Super II's speed, the layout highlighted the introduction of Aurora High Performance Track. Since the days of the vibrators, Aurora had been praised and damned for its track system—great on variety, but deficient in terms of performance. And as car speeds increased, track quality became increasingly important.

Aurora's answer was High Performance Track. Some changes were purely cosmetic, like eliminating the white middle-of-road line found on Aurora track since the days of Highways. Engineers added a deeper slot to accept new blade-style guide pins. Most important was R&D team member Lou Accornero's interlocking-tab track connection system. Finally, an end of Aurora's pins and clips: assembly and disassembly was quicker and sections fit together more precisely, improving performance. 1973's Quikee-Lok tool made assembly even easier.

The most dramatic innovation of High Performance Track was banked curves—something hobbyists had requested for years. Aurora offered four different kinds: Banked S Curve (2543), shallow curves that created twisting "esses" on a straightaway; Hairpin Curve (2544), a steep-bank 6"-radius 180-degree turn; and the 9" Monza Banked Curve and 12" Daytona Banked Curve (2467, 2545), which could be used side by side to make a four-lane track.

Aurora encountered tremendous tooling and manufacturing problems with banked curves—which is why no other company had attempted the products. Indeed, the Hairpin Curve was simply too abrupt, causing cars to fly off at normal speeds. It was discontinued in 1974.

In addition to the Super II and High Performance Track, Aurora had one more 1972 innovation: the Diagnostic Center, four components that helped the slot car hobbyist fine-tune his HO cars. The Weight Analyzer, Power Control, Dyno Tack, and the never-produced Tire Balancer (1546 1544, 1545, 1547) weren't hits with racers like Porcelli

XLerators, the first slotless race cars: Ford J (2743), Cougar (2781), Willys (2782), Vega (2746), Chevy Blazer (2747), #2 Ford GT, #1 Ferrari GTO, Camaro (2741), Firebird (2742), Chaparral 2F (2744).

and designers like Ratkiewich. They considered the devices too crude to be of any value, but Aurora executives insisted they go into production—and that they be inexpensive for toy market appeal. Unfortunately, nobody bought them. Serious racers knew they were useless, and kids who played with slot cars as toys didn't want them.

XLerators: innovation never realized

Since the days when electric slot car sets first achieved success, Aurora designers dreamed of miniature cars running free around the track, unshackled from guide pins and slots. In the early 1970s, Aurora initiated a top-secret program in cooperation with Bell Laboratories to develop a computerized slotless system. Only Jim Keeler and a handful of Aurora executives knew about this "black" project, though it cost Aurora a serious amount of research money. Eventually the effort was abandoned; it offered no realistic hope of a low-cost product.

But innovation was out there, and it emerged from a source Aurora least expected—Montgomery Ward. The retailing giant had been offered a slotless racing concept by an independent toy designer. Ward management went to Aurora and suggested they produce the set as an exclusive for the Ward catalog. Jim Russell, who handled the Ward account, looked over the slotless racing system and pronounced it "Mickey Mouse." However, when Ward insisted they wanted it for their 100th Anniversary Catalog and would pick up initial tooling costs, Aurora went for it.

The result was XLerators. Aurora proclaimed the arrival of "controlled racing," including authentic lane changing and passing. R&D racer

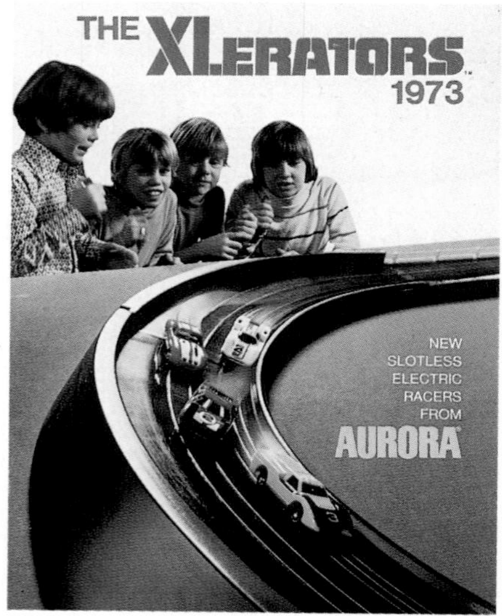

The 1973 launch catalog for XLerators

Porcelli recalls the vast amount of work Aurora put into the system's banked track and electricals, but it never worked properly. The idea was to create a high-speed outer lane and variable-speed inside lane between which the cars would alternate. Unfortunately, the T-jet motor lacked sufficient power to maintain speed, causing the cars to coast between power rails. Worse, the pickup shoes dragged, further slowing the car. With enough deceleration, a car could get stuck between power rails and stall. Once the cars were under way, the only logical strategy was to hold the throttle full open—the high outside lip of the track eliminated wipeouts.

When Aurora showed XLerators at the 1973 HIAA show, Russell installed four power packs in tandem to raise track voltage high enough to keep the cars going. "We were burning up motors right and left," he observed. Aurora, of course, had plenty of spare cars on hand to make up the losses. Would America's kids?

The appropriately named "Demolition Intersection" of 1974 gave the set its only exciting angle. XLerators II, introduced in 1976 with G-Plus motors, promised faster cars and easier setup. However, toy industry journal *Playthings* soon noted the sets' high return rates. XLerators were moderately successful as toys—but they were never taken seriously by hobbyists.

Straightaway fever

As the domain of hardcore motor-tweaking enthusiasts, miniature drag racing had been a part of the slot car scene since its early days. Derek Brand had always opposed drag racer models, feeling there wasn't enough fun in short straightaway races. However, when dragster enthusiast Jim Keeler took A/FX over, drag racers were suddenly considered worthy.

The result: four Dragsters (1772–1774), led by Dodge Fever, named by Keeler after a prize-winning custom model of 1968. The cars were mounted on an AFX specialty chassis, with wide slicks in the rear, a long body extension, and tiny dragster wheels out front. Dragsters didn't do extremely well, but Keeler remained satisfied, noting that the cars added to AFX's rising sales figures.

Aurora's 1974 AFX catalog bore the smiling face of contemporary race car driver Peter Revson, the first celebrity to serve as Aurora spokesman since Dan Gurney and Stirling Moss in 1967. Revson was nephew of president Charles Diker's former boss at Revlon, and Diker knew Revson as a dynamic personality.

However, when Revson came to the Aurora plant at West Hempstead to discuss his role with Aurora, Dick Schwarzchild told him bluntly, "Peter, I'm sorry, but I was involved with this company when Fireball Roberts died, and I don't think [hiring you is] a smart thing to do."

Nevertheless, Revson was hired. He appeared at the HIAA convention in the Aurora suite and was a gracious, unpretentious host of the slot car exhibit. Then on March 21,

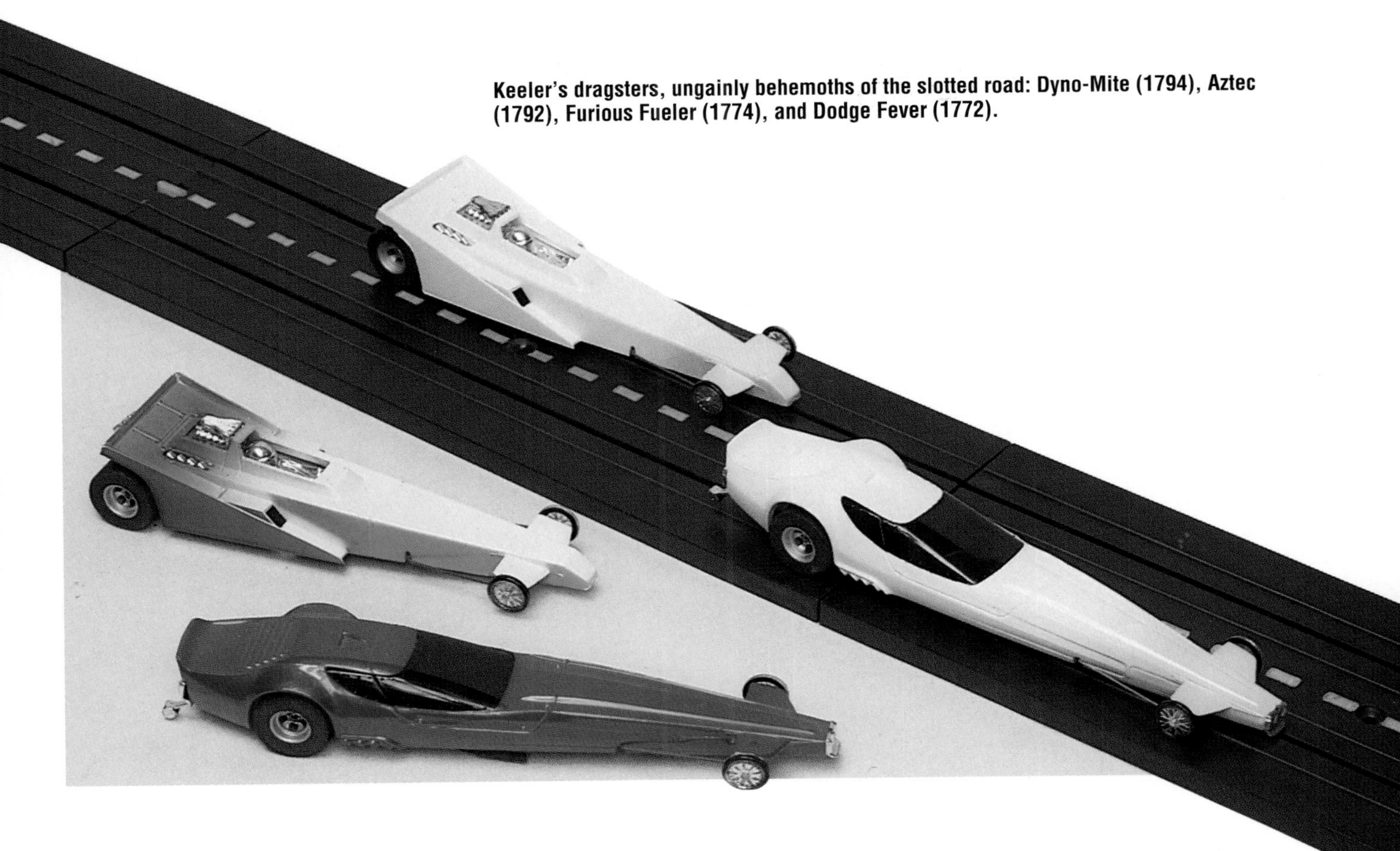

Keeler's dragsters, ungainly behemoths of the slotted road: Dyno-Mite (1794), Aztec (1792), Furious Fueler (1774), and Dodge Fever (1772).

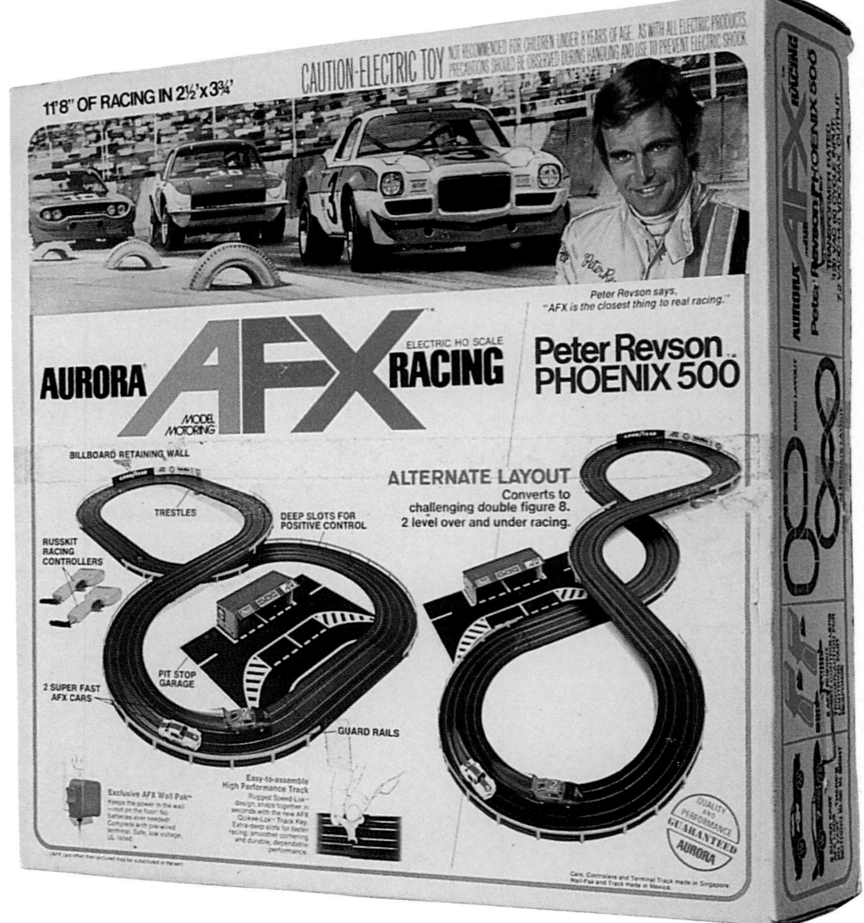

Another ill-fated Aurora celebrity spokesman, Peter Revson, whose image graces only a handful of surviving (and highly collectible) AFX packages.

shortly after Toy Fair, he was killed in a flaming wreck at the South African Grand Prix.

Tens of thousands of AFX set boxes with Revson's picture were tossed into the incinerator, and labels were pasted over his picture on boxes already in the retail pipeline. The Peter Revson case was another lesson not learned.

Aurora's next celebrity spokesman was Jackie Stewart—hired in 1975 only after he had retired from racing and had begun a new career as TV racing commentator. The only question about Stewart was whether his long hair might turn off parents! In 1977 Aurora would take another chance on active drivers, three-time Indy winner A. J. Foyt and six-time NASCAR legend Richard Petty.

By 1974, slot cars had advanced tremendously. They were faster, cornered better, and rode on superior track. But they still sounded like tiny little electrical devices. Aurora tried to solve the problem with "Revamatic Sound." A grandstand unit (1457) with a noise generator wired to the track made noise whenever cars were running. Aurora R&D team member Ken Hill described the sound as "scratchy," thinking it sounded like a little man under the grandstand "banging a drum." It wasn't popular at retail.

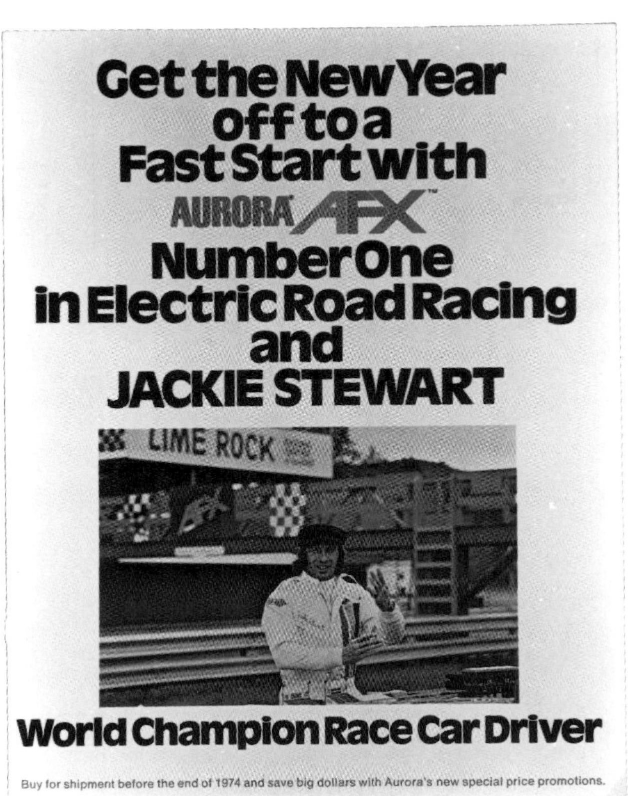

Jackie Stewart, newly retired from racing and unlikely to perish on a racetrack, was a natural for Aurora AFX spokesman.

Magna-Traction Flamethrowers: Porsche 917 (1973), Dodge Charger Daytona (1976), Ferrari 512M (1974), Chevelle stocker (1975).

MAGNETISM

clearly superior

AFX blistercard packaging varied with the prevailing marketing plan.

Time and pressure finally took their toll on Jim Keeler. Early in 1973 he was relieved of responsibility for Aurora's slot car division in order to concentrate on model kits. Keeler had literally worked himself into the hospital from the strain of managing two product lines.

His replacement as AFX product manager was Jim Kirby, who had once thought, "Anybody taking Keeler's job would have to be out of his mind!" Kirby began racing slot cars as a 14-year-old in Los Angeles slot parlors. R&D chief Walter Moe wanted a "hot shot racer" on the staff, and it was soon clear that Kirby's enthusiasm and organizational abilities made him the right choice for the job.

In the hinterlands of club racing, innovation was again rising up from the trenches. In Moosehead, Minnesota, a young man named Tom Bowman began winning races in 1973 with a road-hugging magnetic car that stuck to the track's metal power rails. The concept was simple but incredibly effective, eliminating the need for special brass chassis used by serious racers to lower a car's center of gravity. Bowman's discovery held any car to the road.

At a race in Indianapolis Bowman ran into Ron Esterline and John Snyder, who had independently hit upon the idea of adding magnets to the undersides of their cars. Race officials decided that these innovations constituted an unfair competitive advantage and banned the magnetic cars.

Esterline looked for a way around the ban. He was an old hand at modifying the factory editions offered by Aurora and had won the Indiana state championship of the Grand National back in 1966. Esterline took an AFX chassis, cut the bottom out of the compartments that held the motor magnets, and lowered the magnets nearly to the level of the rails. The magnetic attraction of the motor magnets alone was enough to keep the car on the track.

Aurora was interested enough in what Esterline had done to send a representative out to his garage to inspect his handiwork. Allen McCall, a midwestern enthusiast who wrote a regular column for *Car Model* magazine, shared the secret with the whole slot car world in a February 1974 article.

Purists condemned magnetism as a "gimmick." It decreased the skill demanded of drivers, they argued. Worse, magnetism heightened the already unrealistically fast scale speeds of cars to ridiculous levels. But not everyone was against change. *Car Model*'s Dale Flanagan (November 1973) wrote, "Any HO manufacturer that isn't looking into this with a great deal of seriousness is missing an opportunity to make ready-to-run cars handle as well as any 'pro' HO car."

G-Plus: ahead of the game

What the magazine writers did not know was that Aurora was way ahead of them. In 1972, Jim Russell had been transferred to K&B's Downey, California, plant to head the new Aurora Hobbycrafts division. There he supervised a small team of R&D staff developing new slot car concepts.

Initially, magnetic cars weren't part of the plan. Jim Russell had long felt that for Aurora to maintain its lead, they needed an efficient inline motor/chassis unit to replace the pancake motor and T-jet chassis. His R&D team worked on this concept, led by chief engineer John Wessels. Jack Garcia was the machinist who built the handmade prototypes, and UCLA meteorology

AMC Matador stock car (1930), Chevelle stocker (1929), 1930 Ford Model A coupe (1928), VW Thing (1931), Mercury stocker (1932), Porsche Carrera (1933), Vega funny car (1934).

student Bob Bernhard provided the practicality of an active slot racer.

The three team members went to work on a lightweight racing chassis. The first prototype held a Mabuchi HT-020 motor and didn't perform well, so on the second try Bernhard replaced the Mabuchi magnets with stronger ones from a Versitec motor. To his surprise, the "killer magnets" clamped the chassis to the power rails.

Bernhard walked his prototype—dangling from a section of Aurora track—into Russell's office. "Look at this!" he exclaimed, which produced a collective "ah ha!" from the R&D team.

So arrived the basic concept for Aurora's G-Plus car—and very nearly by accident.

Everyone knew a magnetic car would minimize deslotting and wipeouts—problems that frustrated kids who received Aurora sets for Christmas. Yet there remained major design issues to resolve. The prototype's magnets were so strong, they burned the motor up. Indiana General (Aurora's magnet supplier) sent an engineer to demonstrate how stamped-metal "flux collectors" glued to the bottom of the magnets could focus the magnetism directly onto the rails. Best of all, these weaker magnets were less expensive.

The final product was a revolutionary car. Its in-line motor featured magnets and an armature held together by the plastic chassis itself. Motor magnets rested just above each power rail, and the monocoque chassis was lightweight and fast. In all, a racer's car suitable for mass production.

One phone call from Jim Russell was all it took to get Jim Kirby on a plane to California. He raced a Tuff Ones car against Bernhard and the G-Plus prototype. The superiority of the magnetic car was obvious. A new era in slot car racing had arrived.

Segmenting the line

Despite the obvious superiority of the magnetic car, West Hempstead did not rush it into production. AFX brand manager Jim Kirby had been running slot cars on factory tracks and envisioning the direction of slot car development. Kirby discovered that he enjoyed racing

Vega funny car (1934), Capri funny car (1935), VW Thing roadster (1936), Dodge rescue vehicle (1937), AMC Matador police car (1938), Matador taxi, complete with quarter-panel "dents" (1939), 1956 Ford F-100 pickup (1941), Custom Van (1942), and Ford Street Van (1943).

After years of consumer frustration with slot cars that refused to stay on track, Magna-Traction was the performance innovation Aurora had been seeking.

the older—and slower—Thunderjets more than contemporary AFX cars. Perhaps, he thought, Aurora's quest for speed had taken the fun out of the product. Maybe, he thought, a slower car had more play value. Perhaps, he thought, introducing an even faster car would make slot racing somehow less fun.

Assistant R&D manager Mike Meyers also believed that the Aurora vs. Tyco quest for speed had become "mindless." He thought it ridiculous to pander to the top 2 percent of the market—the hardcore slot racer who bought little of Aurora's product. However, Meyers saw the real benefit of magnetism as he raced with his young son. Kids hated it when their cars flew off the track. A magnetic car was indeed the answer.

Sealing the slow-track fate for Jim Russell's car was Walter Moe. As Aurora's vice president of research and development, Moe knew the new magnetic car would render AFX obsolete, wiping out a generation of investment. Moe felt an evolutionary approach toward magnetic cars would build upon the proven AFX design and be more acceptable to management.

Tony Porcelli was given the unenviable task of designing a magnetic car that used as much AFX tooling as possible. His model had a pancake motor flipped over to lower the center of gravity and position motor magnets as close to the rails as possible. "It was tricky," admitted Porcelli, "but it was manufacturable." Though exceptionally fast, the design would require the major retooling that Aurora wanted to avoid.

Instead, Aurora installed taller magnets in the T-jet motor and lowered them in the chassis. This meant the armature was no longer centered within the magnets, but the motor still worked and, perhaps most important, represented an easy tooling modification.

Aurora AFX cars with Magna-Traction were a Sears exclusive for Christmas 1974 and hit shelves nationwide in 1975. The first G-Plus cars—based on Russell's innovative design—appeared in 1975 as well, hanging on the pegboard next to Magna-Traction AFXs. The low-end market—kids, primarily—would soldier on with the modified AFX cars, while hobbyists would support the new G-Plus design. Aurora even escalated G-Plus pricing to $7.50 when it became obvious that serious racers would pay a premium. After all, nothing from Tyco could catch it.

The pro view

Aurora retained pro slot racers Mike Morrissey, Nick Toma, and Jim Cawthon to conduct a series of independent tests comparing Tyco-Pros, old AFX cars, Magna-Traction AFX cars, and G-Plus cars. Morrissey's confidential report stated, "The introduction of the new cars, particularly the G-Plus, will mark the beginning of a whole new phase of HO scale model car racing. The G-Plus is so good, it's a little eerie."

Morrissey's report declared that even the mainline Magna-Traction cars were "head and shoulders above old-style AFX cars. The TycoPro was the hardest to drive. Its chassis can't cope with its power." TycoPros averaged laps on Morrissey's 32-foot test track at 7.72 seconds, while standard AFXs were marginally faster at 7.57. However, Magna-Traction AFX cars blazed around the course in 6.29, and the G-Plus racers achieved an astounding 5.03 time.

G-Plus bodies were Ron Klein's last contribution to Aurora—and perhaps his best. Accuracy and detail were outstanding. Indeed, the quality of the four G-Plus Formula I cars has never been surpassed by any company since.

Tragically, in the midst of his most creative work, Klein's automobile crashed head-on into another car near West Hempstead. Following a prolonged hospital stay, he was homebound for months. He carved body patterns, then returned to work, but a stroke related to his accident made him an invalid. Klein's departure from Aurora was a true loss to the slot car world.

Nearing the end

The last sets produced by Aurora Products Corporation were unlike any others produced by the slot car pioneer. Screechers and Ultra 5 sets shared more than just variants of the G-Plus motor/chassis—they were both slotless.

The last of Aurora-built AFX, this time called G-Plus: uncataloged mail-in premium #43 Petty Charger—not in the Aurora catalog. Also, Lola T-330 (1731), #2 Ferrari 312 PB (1732), McLaren F-1 (1733), Ferrari F-1 (1734), Indy Special (1735), Ferrari Daytona coupe (1736), Rallye Ford Escort (1737), and Elf F1 (1738).

Screechers was a fully assembled, integrated electrical and track system built into a vacuformed plastic base. Kirby felt it had a great deal of potential: two cars could run simultaneously on the same power strips and, because of the slotless technology, passing was real. Motor magnets (augmented by two more magnets) did a good job of keeping cars on the power rails.

Aurora marketing managers worried that Screechers could steal the low end of the toy market from AFX sets. In a compromise, the four Screechers sets were marketed to younger children through the use of child-appropriate licensing. For

Screechers Spiderman Meets the Fly, a good concept that arrived too late. The box shows the Spider Mobile (5811) and the Fly Mobile (5812).

MODEL MOTORING for 1977
AFX RACING
The New Aurora Racing Team
Jackie Stewart, Richard Petty and A.J. Foyt
AURORA

The final AFX catalog issued by Aurora Products Corporation featured a triple-crown of racing luminaries: Stewart, Petty, and Foyt.

example, the Spiderman Meets the Fly (5757) set required kids merely to install six D-cells, put the cars on track, and turn the throttles.

Aurora Products Corporation's final year is symbolized by its last innovation for the elusive "serious hobbyist" market: Ultra 5, a slotless set with steerable cars. Although the West Hempstead R&D team had labored on the concept for years, it was an outside source—California R&D—that brought the concept to reality. The technology differed from that used with XLerators and Screechers. Ultra 5 eliminated troublesome banked turns and integrated three (rather than two) power rails into each lane. "A" cars ran on the inside and middle rails while "B" cars handled the middle and outside. Either car could run in either lane and, most important, either car could perform realistic passing between lanes. It was the innovation hobbyists had longed for.

Steering was the key to the magic. Ultra 5 cars featured an electromagnetic coil between the two front wheels. The racer's pistol-grip controller featured a tiny steering wheel, recalling the early Aurora controllers. Turning the wheel caused the coil to energize in one direction or another, effecting a lane change. As with any innovation, there were initial problems: the coil drew lots of current and tended to overheat; it took a good bit of practice to control the cars; and most troublesome, the cars were so evenly matched, it was difficult to find the opportunity to pass! But still, Aurora had finally brought true slotless racing to market, and they did it in an evolutionary way that traced its ancestry back to the original vibrators of 1960.

The lasting legacy

Aurora's innovations of the 1970s continued the tradition of technological leadership that had begun in 1960. Without question Aurora sold more slot car sets than any other company in the world. Unfortunately, the robust condition of Aurora's slot car business did not extend to the rest of the corporation.

Aurora began to lose money in

1969. The reason: Aurora's decision to enter the game and toy market. The enormous tooling and television advertising costs simply could not be recouped—even by the high-volume sales that Aurora often enjoyed with smash-hit games like Skittle Bowl. Worse, the oil crisis of 1973–74 sent shock waves through the toy industry; overnight, plastic costs skyrocketed and lowered profit margins across the board.

Changes in the leadership at Aurora parent Nabisco also hastened the West Hempstead firm's demise. Diker had originally courted Nabisco's buyout to gain the capital infusion necessary to underwrite Aurora's move into games and toys. Nabisco president Lee S. Bickmore supported Diker's strategy, but not long after Nabisco's takeover, Bickmore was compelled to retire because of health problems. His successors quickly grew impatient with Aurora's deficits. Overnight, they ceased the capital infusion and accepted a modest profit from the scaled-back company. Diker felt his challenge was gone, and in 1975 he resigned.

Nabisco management retained Boyd Browne from Mattel Toys of Canada to lead Aurora's return to plastic kits and slot cars. "We're concentrating on what we do best," he announced, but it was too late. Nabisco's funding cutbacks were visible everywhere: drastic reductions in games, shrinkage of variety in model kits, and a decline in new slot car body development. Aurora had been rendered a shadow of its former self.

By 1976, many Aurora slot car innovators had left or were laid off. Walter Moe formed his own design company. Jim Keeler and Andy Yanchus, most recently in charge of model kits, were gone. Jim Kirby left early in 1977 to join Moe. Porcelli, Ratkiewich, and Vernon were laid off. When the Aurora Hobbycrafts division was closed in 1974, Jim Russell started his own business.

Ken Hill and Bob Bernhard stayed on through the end of Aurora Products Corporation and into the first years of AFX's new owners. Bernhard's name went on the G-Plus and Magna-Traction patents simply because he was still on staff when patents were applied for.

In the fall of 1976 Nabisco confirmed rumors that Aurora's various divisions were up for sale. In early 1977 Aurora model kit tooling and other assets were bought by Monogram Models. K&B went to Leisure Dynamics and in 1983 was sold to original owner John Brodbeck.

Aurora's remaining division—the jewel in its tarnished crown, AFX slot cars—began a long journey of ownership changes. In November 1977 AFX was purchased by British toy conglomerate Dunbee-Combex-Marx. Overnight, Aurora became a division of Louis Marx & Company. The offices at 44 Cherry Valley Road were cleaned out and locked up. Aurora assets were transferred to Marx headquarters in Stamford, Connecticut. The move was brief; Dunbee-Combex-Marx incurred enormous debts in building its empire, and everything fell apart in 1980.

AFX was purchased by Aurora Canada in 1981 and then in 1984 by Tomy Kogyo Ltd. of Japan. Another change of hands occurred in 1986 when Coleco Industries of Connecticut went looking for a place to invest profits from Cabbage Patch Kids. Coleco purchased Tomy's Canadian and United States divisions, inheriting AFX. However, just two years later, Coleco went into receivership and Tomy resumed ownership of the Aurora AFX slot car line. Today Tomy Aurora AFX sets can be found on the shelves of stores around the world. Aurora slot car veteran Jim Russell is Tomy's AFX national hobby sales representative.

Too much dancing, not enough racing

This catastrophic tangle of events meant that Aurora AFX slot cars and sets lost their leadership role to Tyco. In a final twist of irony, many of the people responsible for Tyco's rise were the same men who had earlier contributed to Aurora's success.

In 1975 Rich Palmer tried to interest Aurora in a revival of the Grand National race series. After a visit to West Hempstead, he wrote a follow-up letter: "It was like old times meeting and working with friendly faces and interesting people." However, Aurora wasn't interested—but Tyco was. Tyco's "Curvehugger Racing Contest" started in 1978 with the same basic rules as the Ford-Aurora Grand National and ran successfully for several years.

Laid off by Nabisco management, Tony Porcelli found employment in Tyco R&D. He recalled an early-1980s meeting when an outside designer demonstrated a new design prototype. It was Derek Brand. His new 440 car could beat AFX's G-Plus. Today the 440's successor, the X2 (another Brand creation) is the ultimate commercial slot car.

Slot cars today are a staple item in hobby shops and toy stores, but they don't enjoy the kind of market share Aurora realized in the 1960s and '70s. Enthusiasm is not lacking, however. Slot car raceways are currently enjoying a revival, and the original generation of Aurora racers—today's adults—collect and race everything from vintage vibrators to Thunderjets and AFXs.

The Aurora story is a classic American tale of toymaking innovation—discovery, meteoric launch, mass enthusiasm, and, ultimately, decline and resurgence. Follow Aurora through the timeline of recent American toy history and you'll find its slot cars defining the toy purchasing habits of two generations. Perhaps most enduring is the fact that Aurora slot cars represent halcyon days of childhood play in a way that no other toy of the time ever could.

PRICE LIST

and photo cross-reference

EACH CAR in this index is identified by its Aurora catalog number. Cars are also cross-indexed by Aurora catalog numbers for other issues of the same body. Also listed are the years the car was depicted in an Aurora catalog. The number after the catalog listing is the page in this book on which a photograph of the car appears.

Known color variations are listed with the predominant body color listed first on any given line, followed by interior color, top color, and stripe or number color, if applicable.

Vibrator and Thunderjet car body patterns were sculpted by Aurora craftsmen Derek Brand, Andrew Yanchus, Lou Crisci, Ron Kohn, and Ron Klein. Several Thunderjet bodies were created by HMS, an independent design shop in Willow Grove, Pennsylvania. When the patternmaker is known, he is identified.

Prices are estimated 1995 retail prices for cars in mint-in-the-box condition. Prices plunge for models in less-than-mint condition. Veteran slot car collectors use a 1–10 scale. A 10 is mint in the box; 9 is mint but unpackaged; 1 is a wreck. Marketplace prices vary.

VIBRATORS

Vibrator bodies attach to the chassis by screw posts at the front and rear. The chassis is die-cast metal. Pickup shoes have U-shaped front ends and are not spring-loaded. The paddle-wheel gear surrounding the rear axle is clearly visible on the chassis underside.

Playcraft Vibrators

Playcraft of England sold two sets: Set 1 containing the Chevy and Ford Lorry; Set 2 containing the Jaguar and Mercedes. Set 1 sells for about $1200 and Set 2 for about $400.

3101 Jaguar XK140, 10

blue	$175
red	$175
dark red	$175
yellow	$175

Issued with slight changes by Aurora as 1541. The clearest difference between the Playcraft Jaguar and Mercedes and their Aurora counterparts are the thin-walled body mounting posts in the Playcraft cars. The colors of the interiors also are not standard Aurora colors. Brand-sculpted body.

3102 Mercedes 300SL, 10

blue	$150
red	$150
white	$150
lemon	$150

Issued with slight changes by Aurora as 1542. Brand-sculpted body.

3103 '58 Chevrolet Impala, 10

blue/white/blue	$700
lime green/red/lime green	$700
orange/white	$700
red/lime green/red	$700
red/white/red	$700
yellow/white/yellow	$700
yellow/black/yellow	$700

Issued by Playcraft in England only. Seven body components made Aurora production unprofitable. Brand-sculpted body.

3104 Ford Lorry, 10

blue	$375
lime green	$375
red	$375
white	$375
white/blue bed	$375

Flatbed truck without side stakes. Dual wheels on rear axle. Issued by Playcraft in England, but not by Aurora in the United States. Brand-sculpted body.

Aurora Vibrators

1541 Jaguar XK140 convertible (1960–62), 11

black/red	$85
blue/black	$75
blue/tan	$75
dark gray/brown	$75
dark gray/red	$75
light gray/red	$75
green/black	$75
green/tan	$75
lemon/red	$60
lemon/tan	$60
red/tan	$60
tan/brown	$60
tan/red	$60
white/black	$60
white/red	$60
white/tan	$60
snow white/red	$60
wine/tan	$85

First issued with slight variations by Playcraft in England. Drivers come in a variety of shirt/cap paint color combinations; some have mustaches! Fold-down top comes in black, tan, red. Brand-sculpted body.

1542 Mercedes 300SL convertible (1960–62), 11

black/brown	$85
black/red	$85
blue/black	$80
dark gray/red	$65
light gray/red	$65
light gray/tan	$65
green/black	$65
lemon/lemon	$60
lemon/red	$60
lemon/tan	$60
red/black	$60
red/tan	$60
tan/red	$60
white/black	$60
white/red	$60
white/tan	$60
snow white/red	$60
wine/black	$75

Some drivers have mustaches. First issued by Playcraft in England. Brand-sculpted body.

1543 1960 Chevrolet Corvette convertible (1960–62), 11

body/side cove/interior colors

black/silver/red	$180
blue/silver/tan	$160
dark gray/silver/black	$125
dark gray/silver/red	$125
light gray/silver/red	$125
metallic gray/silver/black	$150
green/lemon/tan	$150
green/silver/tan	$150
lemon/black/red	$110
lemon/red/red	$125
lemon/silver/red	$125
lemon/tan	$125
red/white/lemon	$125
red/silver/tan	$125
tan/red/red	$125
tan/silver/red	$125
white/black/black	$125
white/black/red	$125
white/silver/red	$125
wine/silver/black	$150
wine/silver/red	$150

Driver figure unique to this car. Three different interiors. Brand-sculpted body.

1544 1960 Ford Thunderbird hardtop (1960–62),11

black/black	$150
black/tan	$155
blue/black	$75
blue/tan	$75
cream/black	$75
dark gray/black	$75
dark gray/tan	$80
light gray/black	$75
light gray/tan	$80
metallic gray/tan	$150
green/black	$75
green/tan	$80
lemon/black	$75
lemon/lemon	$75
lemon/tan	$80

red/black	$75
red/red	$75
red/tan	$80
tan/black	$75
tan/tan	$80
white/black	$75
white/tan	$75
snow white/black	$75
snow white/tan	$75
wine/black	$90
wine/tan	$95

Thunderbird emblem on right rear roof post only. Brand-sculpted body.

1545 Jaguar XK140 coupe (1962), 11

black/red/black	$100
blue/tan/black	$85
blue/tan/tan	$85
dark gray/red/dark gray	$85
light gray/red/black	$85
green/tan/black	$85
green/tan/green	$85
lemon/red/black	$85
lemon/red/lemon	$85
lemon/tan/black	$85
red/tan/black	$85
red/tan/red	$85
tan/red/black	$85
tan/red/tan	$85
white/red/black	$85
wine/tan/black	$100

Brand-sculpted body.

1546 Mercedes 300SL coupe (1962), 11

black/red/black	$100
blue/tan/black	$85
dark gray/red/black	$85
light gray/red/black	$85
green/tan/black	$85
lemon/red/black	$85
lemon/red/lemon	$85
red/black/black	$85
red/black/tan	$85
red/tan/black	$85
red/tan/red	$85
tan/red/black	$85
tan/red/tan	$85
white/red/black	$85
white/red/tan	$85
wine	$85

Brand-sculpted body.

1547 1960 Chevrolet Corvette coupe (1962), 11

body/side/interior/top

black/silver/red/black	$190
blue/silver/tan/black	$160
dark gray/lemon/red/black	$160
dark gray/silver/black/black	$160
dark gray/silver/red/black	$160
light gray/lemon/red/black	$160
light gray/silver/red/black	$160
green/lemon/red/black	$160
green/silver/tan/black	$160
lemon/silver/red/black	$130
lemon/silver/red/lemon	$130
lemon/white/red/black	$130
red/silver/lemon/black	$130
red/silver/tan/black	$130
red/silver/tan/red	$130
red/white/lemon/black	$130
tan/red/red/black	$130
tan/silver/red/black	$130
tan/silver/red/tan	$130
white/black/black/black	$130
white/silver/red/black	$130
white/silver/red/tan	$130
wine/silver/black/black	$160
wine/silver/tan/black	$140

Brand-sculpted body.

1548 1962 Ford Galaxie Sunliner convertible (1962), 11

lemon/black/white	$75
lemon/red/black	$75
lemon/tan/white	$75
red/black/tan	$75
red/tan/black	$75
tan/red/black	$75
tan/black/white	$75
white/black/tan	$75
white/red/black	$75
white/tan/black	$75

Brand-sculpted body. Some Sunliners have been found on a simple plastic chassis, evidently produced as static cars for model railroad layouts.

1549 1962 Ford Galaxie 500 hardtop (1962), 11

lemon/black/black	$75
lemon/red/black	$75
lemon/red/lemon	$75
red/black/black	$75
red/tan/black	$75
red/tan/red	$75
tan/black/black	$75
tan/black/tan	$75
tan/brown/black	$75
tan/red/tan	$75
white/black/black	$75
white/red/black	$75

Brand-sculpted body.

1550 1962 Ford Country Squire station wagon (1962), 14

body/interior/top

lemon/brown/lemon	$100
lemon/red/lemon	$100
lemon/red-lemon/lemon	$100
lemon/tan/lemon	$100
red/tan/red	$100
red/tan-red/red	$100
tan/red/tan	$100
tan/red-tan/tan	$100
white/red/black	$100
white/red-white/black	$100
white/red-white/red	$100

All have light brown/dark brown painted "wood" side panels. Some have two interior colors because only half the interior is painted. Clear top may be painted either on inside or out. Some have painted door handles and tail lights. Brand-sculpted body.

1551 1962 Ford F-100 pickup truck (1962), 14

lemon/lemon/black	$100
lemon/red/black	$100
red/red/black	$100
red/tan/black	$100
tan/red/black	$100
tan/tan/black	$100
white/red/black	$100
white/black/white	$100

Brand-sculpted body.

1552 Ford Galaxie police car (1962), 14

lemon/black/black (police/ two stars)	$120
lemon/black/lemon (police)	$120
lemon/black/white (two stars)	$120
lemon/black/white (police/ two stars)	$120
red/black/black (police/ two stars)	$120
red/black/black (two stars)	$120
red/black/white (police/ two stars)	$120
red/black/white (police)	$120
red/tan/black (police)	$120
red/tan/red	$120
red/black/tan (two stars)	$120
tan/black/black (police)	$120
tan/black/black (two stars)	$120
tan/black/black (police/ two stars)	$120
tan/black/tan (two stars)	$120
tan/black/white (police)	$120
tan/black/white (two stars)	$120
white/black/black (two stars)	$120
white/black/black (police)	$120
white/black/black (police/ two stars)	$120
white/black/white (police/ two stars)	$120

There are two versions of the roof light: early editions have the light molded into the roof and painted red; later editions have a red plastic light glued on. Some variations came without stars; however, stars wear off easily. Brand-sculpted body.

1553 Hot Rod roadster (1962), 14

1365 (Thunderjet 500 version)

black/red	$200
blue/tan	$75
gray/red	$175
green/tan	$75
lemon/black	$75
lemon/red	$75
red/tan	$75
tan/black	$75
tan/red	$75
white/black	$75
white/red	$75

Classic '32 Ford with custom radiator "dreamed up" by sculptor Brand. The two Vibrator hot rods are the only cars with three-spoked wheel hubs. Rear tires are slightly larger than front. Vibrator has four exhaust pipes; T-jet version has only three. Decal sheet with body decorations included in box.

1554 Hot Rod coupe (1962), 14

1366 (Thunderjet 500 version)

body/interior

black/red	$200
blue/tan	$75
gray/red	$175
green/tan	$75
lemon/red	$75
lemon/black	$75
red/tan	$75
tan/red	$75
white/black	$75
white/red	$75

'32 Ford "Deuce Coupe." The two Vibrator hot rods are the only cars with three-spoked wheel hubs. Has four exhaust pipes; T-jet version has only three. Decal sheet with body decorations in box. Brand-sculpted body.

1580 International Semi truck tractor (1962), 14

blue/black	$150
blue/blue	$200
dark gray/black	$150
dark gray/dark gray	$200
light gray/black	$150
light gray/light gray	$200

green/black	$175
green/green	$225
lemon/black	$150
lemon/lemon	$190
red/black	$150
red/red	$190
white/black	$150
white/white	$225
wine/black	$190
wine/wine	$225

Top is usually black; top-body in same color is less common and more valuable. Molded air horn. The pattern for this truck was reworked to become the International Wrecker 1364 (Thunderjet 500 version). Brand-sculpted body.

1582 Mack dump truck (1962), 14

1362 (Thunderjet 500 version)

blue	$95
dark gray	$95
light gray	$95
green	$80
lemon	$80
red	$80
tan	$80
white	$80

Beds are randomly gray or green. Vibrator body cavity has cutout section for motor; T-jet version is solid plastic. Brand-sculpted body.

1583 6-Wheel Mack stake truck (1960–62), 14

1363 (Thunderjet 500 version)

body/bed/stakes	
blue/gray/gray	$100
dark gray/gray/green	$100
dark gray/green/green	$100
light gray/green/green	$100
green/gray/gray	$85
lemon/gray/gray	$85
lemon/green/gray	$85
lemon/green/green	$85
red/gray/gray	$85
red/green/gray	$85
red/green/green	$85
tan/gray/gray	$85
tan/gray/green	$85
tan/green/gray	$85
tan/green/green	$85
white/gray/gray	$85
white/gray/green	$85
white/green/gray	$85
white/green/green	$85

Vibrator body cavity has cutout section for motor; T-jet version is solid plastic. Nine-piece body—the most of any Aurora vehicle. Brand-sculpted body.

1585 Box body trailer (1962), 14

body/frame	
dark gray/dark gray	$15
light gray/light gray	$60
gray/green	$15
green/gray	$15
green/green	$15
olive green/olive green	$30

1586 Van body trailer (1962), 14

gray/gray	$15
gray/gray/Aurora logo	$70
gray/green	$15
green/gray	$15
green/green	$15
green/green/Aurora logo	$70
green/green/Ford logo	$70

THUNDERJETS

Thunderjet bodies attach to the chassis by screw posts at front and rear. Chassis is plastic. Pickup shoes are spring-loaded. Most T-jets came with chrome-plated bumpers, rather than the silver-painted bumpers of the Vibrators. Standard T-jet packaging is a two-piece clear box. Some came in a clear tube with yellow plastic end panels. Some were blistercarded and given stock numbers in the 1100 and 1200 range.

1351 1963 Ford Galaxie convertible (1963–69), 20

body/rugs/seats/boot	
gray/black/red/black	$150
green/black/light green/black	$150
green/light green/black/black	$150
olive green/tan/black/black	$125
olive green/tan/black/tan	$125
lemon/red/black/black	$150
lemon/red/tan/red	$150
red/black/tan/black	$100
red/black/tan/tan	$125
red/gray/black/black	$100
red/tan/black/black	$100
red/tan/black/tan	$100
tan/black/red/white	$100
tan/brown/tan/brown	$100
tan/brown/tan/white	$100
turquoise/black/white/white	$125
turquoise/gray/black/black	$125
white/dark blue/light blue/light blue	$125
white/dark blue/white/black	$100
white/light blue/dark blue/black	$125
white/light blue/dark blue/light blue	$125
white/red/black/black	$100

white/red/black/red	$100
yellow/brown/tan/black	$125
yellow/brown/tan/brown	$125
yellow/brown/white/black	$100
yellow/red/black/black	$100
yellow/red/black/red	$100

Appears in catalog until 1969, but discontinued on sales lists after 1967. Brand-sculpted body.

1352 1963 Ford Galaxie hardtop (1963–69), 20

body/rugs/seats/top

gray/black/red/black	$150
gray/black/red/gray	$150
green/light green/black/black	$150
green/light green/black/green	$150
olive green/tan/black/black	$125
olive green/tan/black/olive green	$125
lemon/red/red/black	$150
lemon/red/tan/red	$150
red/black/tan/black	$100
red/black/tan/red	$125
red/tan/black/black	$100
red/tan/black/red	$125
tan/black/red/tan	$125
tan/brown/tan/brown	$100
tan/brown/tan/tan	$125
tan/red/black/black	$100
turquoise/black/gray/black	$150
turquoise/gray/black/black	$150
turquoise/gray/black/turquoise	$150
white/black/red/red	$100
white/dark blue/light blue/blue	$125
white/dark blue/tan/light blue	$125
white/dark blue/white/light blue	$125
white/light blue/dark blue/light blue	$125
white/light blue/dark blue/white	$125
white/light blue/tan/dark blue	$125
white/red/black/black	$100
yellow/black/red/yellow	$125
yellow/black/tan/black	$125
yellow/brown/tan/yellow	$125
yellow/brown/white/brown	$125
yellow/red/black/black	$100

Appears in catalog until 1969, but disappears from sales lists after 1967. Brand-sculpted body.

1353 1963 Ford Fairlane hardtop (1963–69), 20

body/interior/top

gray/black/gray	$100
gray/red/black	$95
green/black/black	$95
green/black/green	$100
green/light green/black	$95
green/light green/green	$100
olive green/light green/black	$95
olive green/light green/olive green	$95
lemon/red/black	$110
lemon/red/lemon	$110
red/black/red	$95
red/black/black	$75
red/tan/black	$75
red/tan/red	$95
tan/brown/brown	$110
tan/brown/tan	$110
tan/red/black	$95
tan/red/tan	$110
turquoise/black/white	$95
turquoise/gray/black	$95
turquoise/gray/turquoise	$110
white/dark blue/light blue	$110
white/brown/brown	$110
white/red/black	$95
yellow/brown/brown	$95
yellow/brown/yellow	$110
yellow/red/black	$95
yellow/red/yellow	$110

Appears in catalog until 1969, but disappears from sales lists after 1967. Brand-sculpted body.

1354 1963 Ford Falcon hardtop (1963–69), 20

body/interior/top

gray/black/gray	$115
gray/red/black	$90
green/light green/black	$90
green/light green/green	$115
olive green/gray/black	$115
lemon/black/black	$115
lemon/red/black	$115
red/black/black	$90
red/black/red	$115
red/black/tan	$90
red/tan/black	$90
red/tan/red	$115
tan/black/black	$90
tan/black/tan	$115
tan/brown/brown	$90
tan/brown/tan	$115
tan/red/black	$90
turquoise/black/black	$90
turquoise/black/white	$90
turquoise/gray/black	$90

white/dark blue/dark blue	$115
white/dark blue/light blue	$115
white/red/black	$90
white/red/red	$90
yellow/brown/brown	$90
yellow/brown/yellow	$115
yellow/red/black	$90

Brand-sculpted body.

1355 1963 Ford Thunderbird convertible (1963–69), 20

1255 on blistercard.

body/rugs/seats	
slate blue/black/gray	$125
slate blue/red/black	$125
gray/red/black	$140
olive green/black/tan	$70
olive green/tan/black	$70
red/tan/black	$70
tan/brown/black	$70
tan/green/black	$70
tan/red/black	$70
turquoise/gray/black	$70
turquoise/red/black	$70
white/blue/light blue	$70
white/red/black	$70
yellow/brown/black	$70
yellow/red/black	$70

1356 1963 Chevrolet Corvette Stingray (1963–72), 20

1256 on blistercard. 1391 (CC), 6101 (CB), 6801 (SL)

blue	$70
slate blue	$90
gray	$110
green	$50
olive green	$70
red	$50
tan	$50
turquoise	$50
white	$50
yellow	$50

HMS-sculpted body.

1357 1963 Buick Riviera (1963–69), 20

1257 on blistercard. 6109 (CB), 6809 (SL)

blue	$45
slate blue	$110
cream	$45
gray	$110
green	$45
olive green	$45
red	$45
tan	$45
turquoise	$45
white	$45
yellow	$45

Aurora founder Joe Giammarino drove Buicks and was pleased when Buick finally made a hot number suitable for a slot car. Pattern reportedly based on a model kit.

1358 Jaguar XKE coupe (1963–70), 20

1258 on blistercard. 1392 (CC)

black	$95
blue	$40
slate blue	$90
gray	$85
green	$40
olive green	$40
red	$40
tan	$40
turquoise	$40
white	$40
yellow	$40

Brand-sculpted body.

1359 Indianapolis racer (1963–70), 23

1259 on blistercard.

dark blue	$110
cream	$30
gray	$80
lemon	$70
olive green	$80
red	$30
tan	$30
turquoise	$30
white	$30
yellow	$30

numbers: 1, 2, 3, 5, 7, 11, 13
number field: red, white, yellow
number ball: black, red, white
number circle: black, red, white, silver
interior: black, red, wine, white, silver

Designer Brand considered the Indy racer the worst-looking body he ever made for Aurora: "It looked like a fat cigar with wheels!" Bodies were bloated to accommodate the pancake motor. Good seller.

1360 Chrome-plated Indianapolis racer (1965–69), 23

silver	$40
gold	$40

numbers: 1, 2, 3, 5, 7, 11, 13 in white
number ball: black
number circle: red

Same car as 1359. The regular car sold for $2.98; chrome plating boosted the price to $3.49. Brand-sculpted body.

1361 Grand Prix racer (1965–70), 23

1261 on blistercard. 1393 (CC)

green	$55

red $35
tan $35
turquoise $35
white $35
yellow $35
numbers: 2, 3, 5, 6, 7
Cigar-shaped body to accept pancake motor. Model Car & Science (July 1968) called it "100% pure thingie." Appears in 1965 catalog but not on sales lists until 1966. Brand-sculpted body.

1361 International truck trailer (1963)

Listed in the 1963 catalog but never produced. Pairs with the Vibrator International Semi truck tractor (1580), which could not become a T-jet because pancake motor precluded a hitch; the Semi was converted into the Tow Truck (1364).

1362 Mack dump truck (1963–72), 23

1852 (VB)
cab/bed
green/gray $60
olive green/gray $75
olive green/green $75
red/dark gray $60
red/green $60
tan/gray $60
tan/green $60
turquoise/gray $110
turquoise/green $110
white/gray $60
white/green $60
yellow/gray $60
yellow/green $60
To convert from a Vibrator to T-jet made it necessary to widen the body cavity to accept the pancake motor. Cutout in Vibrator body cavity was eliminated.

1363 Mack stake truck (1963–72), 23

1583 (VB)
cab/bed/stakes
green/gray/gray $70
green/gray/green $70
olive green/gray/gray $95
olive green/green/green $95
red/gray/gray $70
red/gray/green $70
red/green/gray $70
red/green/green $70
tan/gray/gray $70
tan/gray/green $70
tan/green/green $70
turquoise/gray/gray $130
turquoise/green/green $130
white/gray/gray $70
white/gray/green $70
white/green/gray $70
white/green/green $70
yellow/gray/gray $70
yellow/gray/green $70
yellow/green/gray $70
yellow/green/green $70
Body cavity widened to convert from vibrator to T-jet. However, the cutout in the Vibrator body cavity was eliminated. Body has more parts than any other T-jet.

1364 International wrecker tow truck (1964–72), 23

body/side stripe
green/black $70
olive green/black $90
red/black $70
tan/red $70
turquoise/black $140
white/red $70
yellow/red $70
Converted from the Vibrator Semi truck tractor (1580). Body cavity widened to convert from a vibrator to T-jet. Usually found with molded cab-roof light (not horn, as in Vibrator version), but a few all-red issues with horn have turned up. Brand-sculpted body.

1365 Hot Rod roadster (1964–72), 24

1265 on blistercard. 1553 (VB)
black/red $150
blue/black $55
gray/black $70
green/black $55
olive green/black $75
olive green/light green $75
red/black $55
red/tan $55
tan/black $55
tan/dark blue $55
tan/brown $55
tan/red $55
turquoise/black $55
white/black $55
white/red $55
yellow/brown $55
yellow/red $55
To convert from a Vibrator into a T-jet the body had to be widened to accept the pancake motor. This was done by eliminating the fourth (rear) exhaust pipe on each side of the body and bulging out the body behind the front wheel well. Has wide racing slick tires in back. Decal sheet. Brand-sculpted body.

1366 Hot Rod coupe (1964–72), 24

1266 on blistercard. 1554 (VB)
black/red $150
blue/black $55

blue/red	$55
gray/black	$70
green/black	$55
olive green/black	$75
olive green/light green	$75
olive green/tan	$75
red/black	$55
red/tan	$55
tan/black	$55
tan/brown	$55
tan/red	$55
turquoise/black	$70
white/black	$55
white/red	$55
yellow/red	$55

To convert from Vibrator, fourth exhaust pipe eliminated and bulge added to body sides behind front wheel well. Wide racing slick tires in back. Decal sheet. Brand-sculpted body.

1367 Maserati (1964–69), 24

1267 on blistercard.

body/stripe

blue	$45
blue/white	$45
green	$45
green/white	$45
olive green	$45
olive green/white	$45
red	$45
red/white	$45
tan	$45
tan/black	$45
turquoise	$45
turquoise/black	$45
white	$45
white/red	$45
yellow	$45
yellow/red	$45
yellow/white	$45

Brand-sculpted body.

1368 Ferrari 250 GTO (1964–70), 24

1268 on blistercard. 1394 (CC), 1493 (FT), 2741 (XL), 6102 (CB), 6802 (SL)

black (painted)/white	$70
blue/white	$40
green/white	$45
olive green/white	$55
red/white	$45
tan/black	$30
turquoise/black	$40
white/red	$30
yellow/red	$30

Brand-sculpted body

1369 '39 classic Lincoln Continental (1965–69), 24

red	$70
tan	$70
turquoise	$70
white	$70
yellow	$70

Appears in 1965 catalog, but not on sales lists until 1966. HMS-sculpted body.

1370 Ford AC Cobra (1965–69), 24

body/rugs/seat

black/red/black (painted)	$150
olive green/gray/black	$125
olive green/light green/black	$120
olive green/tan/black	$120
red/black/gray	$70
red/black/tan	$70
red/tan/black	$70
tan/black/red	$70
tan/brown/tan	$70
tan/brown/white	$70
tan/red/black	$70
turquoise/black/gray	$70
turquoise/black/red	$70
turquoise/gray/black	$70
turquoise/red/black	$70
white/black/red	$70
white/blue/light blue	$70
white/red/black	$70
yellow/black/red	$70
yellow/brown/tan	$70
yellow/green/tan	$70
yellow/red/black	$70

1371 '65 Ford Mustang convertible (1965–69), 29

1271 on blistercard. 6118 (CB), 6818 (SL)

body/rugs/seats/boot/stripe (if any)

black (painted)/red/black/black/white	$180
blue/black/gray/black/white	$150
slate blue/red/black/black	$175
green/black/gray/black/white	$110
olive green/black/light green/black	$170
olive green/black/light green/light green	$170
olive green/black/light green/olive green	$170
olive green/black/light green/black/white	$170
red/black/tan/black	$55
red/black/tan/black/white	$55
red/black/tan/red	$60
red/tan/black/black	$55
red/tan/black/tan	$60

tan/black/red/black	$55
tan/black/red/black/black	$55
tan/black/red/brown	$60
tan/brown/tan/brown	$60
tan/brown/tan/brown/black	$55
tan/red/black/black	$55
tan/red/black/red	$60
turquoise/black/gray/black/ black	$55
turquoise/black/gray/black	$55
turquoise/gray/black/black	$55
turquoise/gray/black/ black/black	$55
turquoise/gray/black/ turquoise	$55
white/black/red/black	$55
white/black/red/black/black	$55
white/blue/light blue/ light blue	$70
white/red/black/black	$55
white/red/black/black/red	$55
white/red/black/red	$65
white/red/black/white	$65
yellow/black/red/black	$70
yellow/black/red/black/red	$55
yellow/brown/tan/brown	$60
yellow/red/black/black	$55
yellow/red/black/black/red	$55

Brand-sculpted body.

1372 '65 Ford Mustang coupe (1965–69), 29

1272 on blistercard.

black (painted)/red/black/ black/white	$180
blue/black/gray/black/white	$150
slate blue/red/gray/black (not a production car)	
green/black/gray/black/ white	$125
green/black/gray/green/ white	$110
olive/black/gray/black/ white	$125
olive green/black/light green/black	$110
olive green/black/light green/black/white	$110
olive green/black/light green/light green	$125
olive green/black/light green/olive green	$110
olive green/black/tan/ olive green	$125
red/black/tan/black	$55
red/black/tan/black/white	$55
red/black/tan/red	$60
red/black/tan/red/white	$60
red/tan/black/black	$55
red/tan/black/red	$60
red/white/black/black	$55
tan/black/red/black/black	$55
tan/black/red/black	$60
tan/black/red/brown	$60
tan/brown/tan/brown	$60
tan/brown/tan/tan	$60
tan/brown/tan/brown/black	$55
tan/red/black/black	$55
tan/red/black/tan	$60
turquoise/black/gray/black	$55
turquoise/black/gray/black/ black	$55
turquoise/black/gray/ turquoise/black	$60
turquoise/gray/black/black	$55
turquoise/gray/black/ turquoise	$60
white/black/red/black	$55
white/black/red/white	$60
white/black/red/black/black	$55
white/dark blue/light blue/ white	$75
white/blue/light blue/ light blue	$75
white/red/black/black	$55
white/red/black/black/red	$60
white/red/black/white	$60
white/red/black/light blue/ red	$75
yellow/black/red/black	$55
yellow/black/red/black/red	$55
yellow/black/red/yellow	$60
yellow/brown/tan/brown	$60
yellow/red/black/black	$55

Brand-sculpted body.

1373 '65 Ford Mustang 2+2 (1966–70), 29

1173 on blistercard. 1416 (WO), 1501 (special issue)

body/rugs/seats/top/stripe

black (painted)/red/black/ black/white	$180
blue/black/gray/blue/white	$150
green/black/gray/green/ white	$110
olive green/black/gray/olive green/white	$150
red/black/tan/red/white	$50
red/tan/black/red	$50
red/tan/black/red/white	$50
red/white/black/red	$50
tan/black/red/tan/black	$50
tan/brown/tan/tan/black	$50
turquoise/black/gray/ turquoise/black	$50
turquoise/gray/black/	

turquoise/black	$50
white/black/red/white	$50
white/black/red/white/black	$50
white/red/black/white/red	$50
yellow/black/red/yellow/red	$50
yellow/red/black/yellow/red	$50

Brand-sculpted body. Special Candy Colored Mustangs (1501) were issued for use in the Third Ford/Aurora Grand National Championship. Two cars came packaged with "tire trac" liquid, screwdriver, controller, license plate. Individual cars: $400. Complete boxed set: $1,000. Candy Colors (painted): blue, green, or red/silver stripe.

1374 Ford GT (1966–72), 43

1274 on blister card. 1395 (CC), 1417 (WO), 1472 (TO), 1494 (FT), 2742 (XL), 6105 (CB), 6805 (SL).

body/stripe

black/white	$70
blue	$30
blue/black	$30
blue/white	$30
medium blue/black	$30
green/black	$30
green/white	$30
olive green/black	$40
olive green/white	$40
red/black	$30
red/white	$30
tan/black	$30
tan/brown	$30
turquoise/black	$30
white/black	$30
white/dark blue	$30
white/red	$30
yellow/black	$30

Real Ford GT-40 premiered at LeMans 1965. This slot car body appeared in more Aurora issues than any other body. Crisci-sculpted body.

1375 Cobra GT (1966–72), 43

1275 on blistercard. 1396 (CC), 6113 (CB), 6813 (SL)

black (painted)/white	$70
blue/white	$30
green/white	$30
olive green/black	$40
olive green/white	$40
red/white	$30
tan/black	$30
turquoise/black	$30
white/black	$30
white/dark blue	$30
white/red	$30
yellow/black	$30

Crisci-sculpted body.

1376 Porsche 906 (1966–70), 43

1276 on blistercard. 6112 (CB), 6812 (SL)

black (painted)/white	$70
blue/white	$30
green/white	$30
olive green/white	$30
red/white	$30
tan/black	$30
turquoise/black	$30
white/red	$30
yellow/black	$30
yellow/red	$30

Yanchus- and Crisci-sculpted body.

1377 Chevrolet Chaparral (1966–72), 43

1277 on blistercard. 6114 (CB)

black (paint) no number	$90
blue	$40
green	$40
olive green	$45
red	$40
tan	$40
turquoise	$40
white	$40
yellow	$40

numbers: 2, 3, 5, 7

Car received criticism because its silhouette does not match that of the real race car, supposedly because Aurora sculptors worked from a photo that distorted the car's shape. Ray Hoy of Model Car & Track (June 1966) liked the body: "It is very well proportioned, one of the very best HO cars I have seen so far." Crisci-sculpted body. Early issues have roll bars; later do not.

1378 Lola GT (1966–70), 43

1278 on blistercard. 1471 (TO), 6106 (CB), 6806 (SL)

body/stripe(s)

black/white/red (painted)	$70
blue/white	$30
green/white	$30
olive green/silver/black	$40
red/silver/black	$30
red/white	$30
red/white/black	$30
tan/white/black	$30
turquoise/black	$30
turquoise/white/black	$30
turquoise/white/red	$30
white/black	$30
white/red	$30
white/red/black	$30
yellow/black	$30
yellow/black/white	$30
yellow/red	$30

Crisci-sculpted body.

1379 Oldsmobile Toronado (1966–70), 43
6108 (CB)

black (painted)	$100
black	$70
blue	$50
green	$50
olive green	$70
red	$50
turquoise	$50
tan	$50
white	$50
yellow	$50

Appears in 1970 catalog, but dropped from sales lists after 1969. Crisci-sculpted body.

1380 Chevrolet Mako Shark (1967–72), 43
1280 on blistercard. 6103 (CB), 6803 (SL)

black (painted)	$90
blue	$45
brown	$80
green	$45
olive green	$60
light orange	$75
red	$45
tan	$45
turquoise	$45
white	$45
yellow	$45

Later editions in brown and orange have larger wheel wells; mold had been modified to produce Flashback cars. Yanchus- and Crisci-sculpted body.

1381 Dino Ferrari (1967–72), 43
1281 on blistercard. 1481 (TO), 6111 (CB), 6811 (SL)

black (painted)/white	$60
blue/white	$30
green/white	$30
olive green/white	$40
red/white	$30
tan/black	$30
turquoise/black	$30
white/red	$30
yellow/red	$30

Yanchus-sculpted body.

1382 Ford "J" (1967–72), 43
1282 on blistercard. 1430 (FT), 2743 (XL), 6104 (CB), 6804 (SL)

black/white	$50
black (painted)/white	$50
blue/black	$30
green/black	$30
olive green/black	$40
red/black	$30
tan/brown	$30
turquoise/black	$30
white/black	$30
white/blue	$30
yellow/black	$30
yellow/blue	$30

Yanchus-sculpted body.

1383 '67 Ford Thunderbird coupe (1967–69), 43
1283 on blistercard. 1502 (special issue), 6110 (CB), 6810 (SL)

green	$70
red	$55
tan	$55
turquoise	$55
white	$55
yellow	$55

Chrome-plated special edition (1502, $400) was sold only in hobby shops that participated in the Fifth Ford-Aurora Grand National. Yanchus-sculpted body.

1384 Green Hornet's Black Beauty (1967–69), 40
1284 on blistercard.

black/green sticker	$190

Customized Chrysler Imperial, the only four-door T-jet. $3.49 price versus $2.98 regular Aurora price. Yanchus-sculpted body; he explained that because of its bulk, the Black Beauty was one of the few bodies that didn't have to be distorted to accept a T-jet motor.

1385 Batmobile (1967–70), 40
1285 on blistercard.

black/red	$190

$3.49 price. Brand-sculpted body.

1386 '67 Ford XL 500 (1967–70), 38
1503 (special issue), 6107 (CB), 6807 (SL)

blue	$60
green	$60
red	$60
tan	$60
turquoise	$60
white	$60
yellow	$60

Chrome-plated special edition (1503, $400) was sold only in hobby shops that participated in the Fifth Ford-Aurora Grand Nationals. Yanchus-sculpted body.

1387 Thunderbike (1967–70), 38
1287 on blistercard.

bike/driver	
blue-black/blue-black	$55
blue-silver/blue-black	$55
red-black/red-black	$55

red-black/white-black $55
red-black/yellow-black $55
red-white/white-black $55
red-silver/red-black $55
red-yellow/yellow-black $55
wine-black-silver/wine-black $70

A Derek Brand creation. 1/48 scale bike based on a Honda. Powered by a T-jet motor mounted sideways. Stabilized by pickup shoes extending from the sides far enough to make contact with the track power rails. Performed well on straights but was top-heavy on curves. Since the driver was attached to the bike by his hands, wipeouts caused him to fly head over heels! The Thunderbike race set (1319) appeared only in the 1967 catalog, but the individual bikes were carried through 1970. "Service Kit" (8740) included replacement body, handle bars, front fender, headlight blistercarded on a card.

1388 '67 Chevrolet Camaro (1968–70), 38

1418 (WO), 1480 (TO), 2741 (XL), 6115 (CB), 6815 (SL)

black/white $80
blue/black $55
blue/white $55
brown/gold $100
green/black $55
green/white $55
lime green/green $100
red/black $55
tan/black $55
turquoise/black $55
white/black $55
yellow/black $55

Pattern was also used for the Pontiac Firebird (1402), just like the real GM cars. After much use, the Camaro side cam tools were damaged and replaced by Pontiac tools. Pontiac had rocker panel trim, left in place on later Camaros—thus Camaros found today with and without rocker panel lines. Kohn-sculpted body.

1389 '67 Mercury Cougar (1968–70), 38

1289 on blistercard. 1419 (WO), 1479 (TO), 2781 (XL), 6116 (CB), 6816 (SL)

black $65
blue $35
green $35
red $35
tan $35
turquoise $40
white $40
yellow $35

Kohn- and Yanchus-sculpted body.

CANDY-COLORED THUNDERJETS

Between 1966 and 1969, six regular T-jet cars were issued with special metallic-colored bodies. The early issues were painted; later issues were plated. These cars sold for $3.49 when regular T-jets sold for $2.98.

1391 Candy-Colored Corvette Sting Ray (1966–69), 31

1356 (Thunderjet 500 version)
Painted: blue, green, red $100
Plated: blue, copper, green, peach, purple, red $75

1392 Candy-Colored Jaguar XKE (1966–69), 31

1358 (Thunderjet 500 version)
Painted: blue, green, red $90
Plated: blue, copper, green, peach, purple, red $55

1393 Candy-Colored Grand Prix racer (1966–69), 31

1361 (Thunderjet 500 version)
Painted: blue #3, green #2, red #7 $70
Plated: blue #3, copper #2, green #2, peach #3, peach #7, purple #3, red #7 $55

All have silver stripes.

1394 Candy-Colored Ferrari 250 GTO (1966–69), 31

1368 (Thunderjet 500 version)
Painted: blue, green, red $70
Plated: blue, copper, green, peach, purple, red $55

1395 Candy-Colored Ford GT (1966–69), 31

1374 (Thunderjet 500 version), 1417 (WO), 1472 (TO), 1494 (FT), 2742 (XL)
Painted: blue, green, red $70
Plated: blue, copper, green, peach, purple, red $45

All have silver stripes.

1396 Candy-Colored Cobra GT (1966–69), 31

1375 (Thunderjet 500 version)
Painted: blue, green, red $70
Plated: blue, copper, green, peach, purple, red $45

All have silver stripes.

1397 McLaren-Elva (1968–72), 47

1297 on blistercard. 1431 (FT), 6117 (CB)

blue/white $35
green/white $35
red/white $35

tan/white	$50
turquoise/white	$35
white/red	$35
yellow/red	$35

Yanchus-sculpted body.

1398 Dune Buggy roadster (1969–72), 47

1298 on blistercard.

blue	$40
green	$40
lime green	$60
purple	$60
red	$40
turquoise	$40
white	$40
yellow	$40
medium blue	$40
orange	$40

Yanchus-sculpted body.

1399 Dune Buggy coupe (1969–72), 47

1299 on blistercard. 1473 (TO)

blue	$40
medium blue	$70
green	$40
lime green	$70
light orange	$70
purple	$70
red	$40
turquoise	$40
white	$40
yellow	$40

All tops are red/white. Yanchus-sculpted body.

1400 Mangusta Mongoose (1969–72), 47

1100 on blistercard. 6120 (CB), 6820 (SL)

blue	$40
light blue	$75
butterscotch	$75
green	$40
lime green	$75
red	$40
turquoise	$40
white	$40
snow white	$40
yellow	$40

Only T-jet with colored chrome. Yanchus-sculpted body.

1401 Willys "Gasser" (1969–72), 48

1101 on blistercard. 1474 (TO), 2782 (XL)

blue	$50
green	$50
red	$50
white	$50
snow white	$50
yellow	$50

Drag racing side panel decals on early issues. Yanchus-sculpted body.

1402 '68 Pontiac Firebird (1969–72), 51

1102 on blistercard. 1478 (TO), 2742 (XL)

blue	$50
green	$50
red	$50
white	$50
snow white	$50
yellow	$50

Much of the pattern used to make the mold for this car body was shared with the Camaro (1388). Kohn- and Yanchus-sculpted body.

1403 Cheetah (1969–72), 51

1103 on blistercard. 1475 (TO)

blue	$40
green	$40
red	$40
white	$40
yellow	$40

Yanchus-sculpted body.

1404 Volkswagen with Flower Power (1969–72), 51

1104 on blistercard. 1482 (TO)

Decorated with flowers with either rounded or pointed petals.

blue/white pointed	$45
blue/white rounded	$45
green/white pointed	$45
green/white rounded	$45
lemon/red rounded	$120
red/white pointed	$45
red/white rounded	$45
white/green pointed	$45
white/green rounded	$45
snow white/red rounded	$70
yellow/red pointed	$45
yellow/red rounded	$45

Copied from Faller's VW.

1405 Formula I McLaren BRM (1969–72), 51

1105 on blistercard.

red #11	$40

The slim-line T-jet motor was designed to fit into the special narrow chassis of this Formula I car. It sold at $4 when T-jets were $3. Slim-line cars weren't as fast as regular T-jets, and motors ran hotter.

1406 Formula I Repco Brabham (1969–72), 51

1106 on blistercard.

green #2	$40

Slim-line motor. $4 car. The real car won the World Championship in 1966 and 1967. Yanchus-sculpted body.

1407 '68 Dodge Charger (1969–72), 48

1107 on blistercard.

black/white	$300
blue/black	$125
gray/black	$190
green/black	
light green/black	$150
lime green/black	$150
olive drab/black	$150
lemon/black	$125
orange/black	$220
purple/black	$220
purple/white	$220
red/black	$100
turquoise/black	$100
white/black	$100
snow white/black	$120
snow white/red	$120
yellow/black	$100

Aurora acquired one delivery of olive-drab plastic, which it used on this car only. HMS-sculpted body.

1408 '68 Ford Torino (1969–72), 48

1108 on blistercard.

black/gold	$70
black/white	$70
green/gold	$70
green/white	$70
red/white	$55
white/red	$55
yellow/black	$55

HMS-sculpted body.

1409 Alfa Romeo Type 33 (1969–72), 49

1109 on blistercard.

body/rollbar	
blue/blue	$45
blue/chrome	$45
green/green	$45
green/chrome	$45
red/red	$45
red/chrome	$45
tan/chrome	$45
white/white	$45
white/chrome	$45
yellow/yellow	$45
yellow/chrome	$45

$3.50 when other cars sold for $3. Race decals on the sides. Yanchus-sculpted body.

1410 Chaparral 2F (1970–72), 49

1110 on blistercard. 1476 (TO), 2744 (XL)

white/black #1	$35

HMS-sculpted body.

1411 '69 Pontiac GTO (1972), 49

1111 on blistercard.

medium blue/black	$135
brown/black	$110
brown/brown	$110
brown/brown/silver stripes	$160
butterscotch/black	$160
red/black	$135
snow white/black	$135

Appears only in 1972 catalog, but appears on sales lists in 1971–72. HMS-sculpted body.

1414 '69 American Motors AMX (1970–72), 49

1114 on blistercard.

medium blue/white	$55
lime green/black	$70
lemon/black	$70
orange/mustard	$70
white/black	$70
white/red	$55

HMS-sculpted body. Typically HMS produced patterns in exact HO scale, but this car received three-times HO treatment. Produced at a time when Aurora was trying to upgrade detail level; one of the best T-jet bodies.

1415 '69 Ford Mustang Mach I (1970–72), 49

1115 on blistercard.

blue	$140
medium blue	$135
red	$140
white	$115
yellow	$115

HMS-sculpted body.

THE WILD ONES

In 1969 and 1970, four regular T-jet cars were issued in snow-white plastic with racing stripes. Special tires and a decal sheet came with each. Cars feature modifications to increase speed. $4 when regular T-jets sold for $3. Packaged in a clear box with white end caps.

1416 Wild Mustang 2 + 2 (1969–70), 50

1373 (Thunderjet 500 version)

snow white/red #7	$60

1417 Wild Ford GT (1969–70), 50
1374 (Thunderjet 500 version), 1395 (CC), 1472 (TO), 1494 (FT), 2742 (XL)
snow white/orange/ black #5 $35

1418 Wild Camaro (1969–70), 50
1388 (Thunderjet 500 version), 1479 (TO), 2741 (XL)
snow white/blue #2 $50

1419 Wild Cougar (1969–70), 50
1389 (Thunderjet 500 version), 1479 (TO), 2781 (XL)
snow white/red #3 $45

1421 '32 Ford pickup (1970–72), 51
1121 on blistercard.

medium blue	$120
lime green	$120
lemon	$120
orange	$120
red	$120

Body copied from a Lindberg "Mini Lindy" model kit. Slim-line T-jet motor. $4 when other cars sold for $3.50.

1429 Chevrolet El Camino (1970–72), 51
1129 on blistercard.

blue	$140
red	$140
turquoise	$110
white	$100
yellow	$100
yellow/black top	$120

Surfboards in turquoise, white, yellow. HMS-sculpted body.

1483 "Sand Van" Dune Buggy (1971–72), 59
1183 on blistercard. 1496 (FT)

light blue/white	$45
lime green/white	$35
orange/white	$45
pink/white	$35

Ratkiewich's first project at Aurora was to design a simple part to add to the Dune Buggy roadster (1398) so it could go into a low-cost toy set.

1484 Super modified roadster (1971–72), 59
1184 on blistercard. 1553 (VB), 1365 (Thunderjet 500 version)

medium blue	$170
bright yellow	$170
bright orange	$170

Spoiler and side pipes were added to the old Hot Rod roadster, resulting in this dirt-track racer.

1485 "Bushwhacker" Snowmobile (1971–72), 59
1185 on blistercard.

body/driver	
blue/blue	$35
medium blue/lemon	$35
blue/butterscotch	$35
butterscotch/blue	$35
butterscotch/lemon	$35
lemon/medium blue	$35
lemon/lemon	$35
white/blue	$50

Simple mold designed by Ratkiewich for low-cost toy set.

1487 Good Humor ice cream truck (1972), 59

white/Good Humor labels	$30
white/Good Humor & Wild Huckleberry labels	$45

Last of the Thunderjets. Klein-sculpted body.

THUNDERJET FLAMETHROWERS

In 1970 Aurora introduced cars with headlights and tail lights to enhance their appeal as toys. They were marketed with the "24 Hours of Le Mans" (1323) race set, which attempted a realistic portrayal of nighttime driving. The "Flamethrowers" cost $4 compared to $3 for regular T-jets. Individual cars sold in a special box with white plastic base and clear, rounded top.

1430 Flamethrower Ford "J" (1970–72), 51
1130 on blistercard. 1382 (Thunderjet 500 version), 2743 (XL)
white/blue $30

1431 Flamethrower McLaren Elva (1970–72), 51
1131 on blistercard. 1397 (Thunderjet 500 version)

black/white	$30
blue/white	$45
green/white	$45
red/white	$45

1491 Flamethrower Chaparral 2F (1971–72)
1191 on blistercard. 1410 (Thunderjet 500 version)

white/black	$35
snow white/black #7	$30
snow white/blue #7	$35
snow white #1	$30

1493 Flamethrower Ferrari (1971–72)
1193 on blistercard. 1368 (Thunderjet 500 version), 2741 (XL)

medium blue/white	$35
red/white	$35

1494 Flamethrower Ford GT (1971–72)

1194 on blistercard. 1374 (Thunderjet 500 version), 1395 (CC), 1417 (WO), 1472 (TO), 2742 (XL)

light blue	$30
light blue/black	$30
light blue/orange/black #5	$30
brown/white	$30

1495 Flamethrower Cobra GT (1971–72)

1195 on blistercard. 1374 (Thunderjet 500 version)

blue/white	$30
dark brown	$30

1496 Flamethrower "Sand Van" Dune Buggy (1971–72)

1196 on blistercard. 1483 (Thunderjet 500 version)

lime green/green	$35
pink/purple	$35

TUFF ONES

Aurora introduced the Tuff Ones in 1970—regular T-jet bodies with improvements to the motor, chassis, and tires. Bodies have new, brighter plastic colors and more elaborate body detail painting. They come in distinctive boxes with a white base and clear plastic dome.

1471 Tuff Ones Lola GT (1970–72), 52

1378 (Thunderjet 500 version)

black (came in package with 1477)	$90
black/pink/white-black #3	$30
lemon/pink/white-black #3	$45
dark yellow/pink/ white-black #3	$30

1472 Tuff Ones Ford GT (1970–72), 52

1374 (Thunderjet 500 version), 1395 (CC), 1417 (WO), 1494 (FT), 2742 (XL)

blue/black	$30
light blue (came in package with 1478)	$90
light blue/orange-black #5	$40
red/black	$30

1473 Tuff Ones Dune Buggy coupe (1970–72), 52

1399 (Thunderjet 500 version)

lemon/blue-white	$35
lemon/no top (came in package with 1479)	$90

1474 Tuff Ones Willys "Gasser" (1970–72), 52

1401 (Thunderjet 500 version), 2782 (XL)

lemon/purple	$50
lemon/plum	$60
lemon (came in package with 1480)	$90

1475 Tuff Ones Cheetah (1970–72), 52

1403 (70–72)

orange #2	$35
orange (came in package with 1481)	$90

Several unusual colored Cheetahs have turned up; possible factory test runs.

1476 Tuff Ones Chaparral 2F (1970–72), 52

1410 (Thunderjet 500 version)

lime green/blue #7	$35
white (came in package with 1482)	$90
white/black #7	$30
white/blue #7	$30

1477 Tuff Ones AMX (1971–72), 52

1414 (Thunderjet 500 version)

red/white-blue #5	$35
red/silver #5	$25
white/blue #5	$25

1478 Tuff Ones Firebird (1971–72), 52

1402 (Thunderjet 500 version), 2742 (XL)

dark yellow/black	$40
dark yellow/black #7	$40
light yellow/black	$40
light yellow/black #7	$40
red/white painted bumpers	$35
snow white	$40
snow white/red	$40
snow white/red #7/painted bumpers	$40
snow white/red #7/plated bumpers	$40

Dark yellow and light yellow versions may be unplanned variations from the molding process.

1479 Tuff Ones Cougar (1971–72), 52

1389 (Thunderjet 500 version), 1419 (WO), 2781 (XL)

snow white/butterscotch #21	$35

1480 Tuff Ones Camaro (1971–72), 52

1388 (Thunderjet 500 version), 1418 (WO), 2741 (XL)

blue/yellow #1	$40

1481 Tuff Ones Dino Ferrari (1971–72), 52
1381 (Thunderjet 500 version)
red/green/white #3 $25

1482 Tuff Ones Volkswagen (1971–72), 52
orange/white/black #2/ yellow tinted windows $40
orange/white/black #2/green tinted windows $40

AFX SUPER II

In 1972 and 1973 Aurora offered an HO slot car which incorporated all the hop-up techniques used by pro slot racers. The body is vacuformed and attaches to the chassis front with pins. Long lead weights are slung under the nose and along chassis sides. 1972 issues have braided pickups; 1973 have regular pickup shoes.

1788-880 Super II (1972–73)
red-orange #4 $100

1788-881 Super II (1973), 56
mustard #4 $100

The following two cars appear in Aurora catalogs, but probably were not issued.

1788-882 Super II (1973)
blue #1

1788-883 Super II (1973)
white/red stripes #3

AFX

The first AFX cars were introduced in 1971. Some Thunderjet cars stayed in the Aurora catalog in 1971 and 1972, but by 1973 all Aurora cars were AFX. In 1975 Magna-Traction cars appeared, and most of the earlier AFX cars were converted. AFX bodies snap onto the plastic chassis. Pickup shoes are spring loaded. Post-1972 cars have soft rubber rear tires. All but a few AFX car body patterns were either sculpted by Ron Klein or designed by staff artists Richard Ratkiewich, John Vernon, and Ken Hill for production by outside pattern shops.

1702 Grand Am funny car (1974), 56
1926 (MT)
blue/yellow/red $75
white/red/medium blue $25
yellow/orange $30
Ratkiewich-designed body.

1703 Corvette "A" production (1974), 56
1927 (MT)
black/yellow $60
bright yellow/black $25
Ratkiewich-designed body.

1745 Datsun Baja pickup (1974), 56
1919 (MT)
blue/black #211 $25
mustard $30
mustard #211 $25
lemon yellow/black $30
lemon yellow/black #211 $20
Klein-sculpted body.

1746 1929 Model A Woody (1974), 56
1920 (MT)
black/mustard/brown "wood" side panels$20
Different version of 1791, 1928. Vernon-designed body.

1747 Porsche 917-10K Can-Am (1974), 56
1921 (MT), 3001 (U5)
white/blue-red #16 (round front) $20
white/blue-red #16 (square front) $35
white/blue-red #23 $60
RC Cola logo on nose and spoiler. RC Cola sold sets as premiums. Real car driven by Charlie Kemp in the 1972 Can-Am season. Car Model (November 1973) called it "the best model yet . . . bar none!" Klein-sculpted body.

1748 Dodge Street Van (1974), 56
1922 (MT)
lime green/medium blue $20
opaque green/medium blue $30
yellow/orange $20
orange/black $20
"Specialty Chassis" like 1781 Roarin' Rolls. Ratkiewich-designed body.

1751 Ferrari Can-Am 612 (1971–74), 56
(RB)
bright blue #15 $20
bright orange #15 $20
red #15 $20
bright yellow/purple #15 $20
bright yellow/red #15 $20
Klein-sculpted body.

1752 Auto World McLaren XLR (1971–74), 56

(RB)

bright blue #54	$35
bright blue/black #54	$30
bright orange/black #54	$30
bright orange/dark blue #7	$65
bright orange/gray #54	$25
bright yellow #54	$30

Number 54 was the car sponsored by Auto World and driven by editor Oscar Koveleski. Koveleski was active in the slot car hobby. His father Anthony Koveleski had been a pioneer in wood and plastic scale model cars in the 1940s and '50s. Klein-sculpted body.

1753 Dodge Daytona Charger (1971–74), 59

1900 (MT)

bright blue/black #7	$35
orange/black #7	$40
red/black #7	$200
bright yellow/black #7	$30
lemon yellow/black #7	$30

Klein-sculpted body.

1754 "Too Much" (1971–74), 59

5788, 5812 (SC)

lime green/blue green	$35
lime green/green & gold metallic	$35
lime green/green & silver metallic	$35
bright orange/purple	$30
red/black	$35
lemon yellow/black	$25
lemon yellow/orange	$25

Larger scale version used in Powerslicks 2151. HMS-designed body.

1755 "Turbo Turnon" (1971–74), 59

5787, 5811 (SC)

bright orange/purple/yellow chrome	$25
white/red/blue stars	$25
yellow/blue	$25
lemon yellow/blue	$25

Larger scale version used in Powerslicks 2152. This and "Too Much" were issued as a quick, inexpensive add-ons to the then-small A/FX line. Aurora toolmakers reduced Powerslicks bodies. "I hated 'em," declared product manager Keeler. He referred to this car as the "Terrible Turnoff." They were the last of the "thingie" bodies. Slowest selling of the first AFX cars. HMS-designed body.

1756 Trans-Am Camaro Z-28 (1971–74), 59

1901 (MT)

light blue/purple #3	$30
white/medium blue #3	$25
white/orange #3	$60

Klein-sculpted body.

1757 Porsche 917 (1971–74), 59

1902 (MT), 1798 (AFT), 1973 (AFT)

light blue/orange #2	$25
white/purple #2	$20
bright yellow/medium blue #2	$15

Gulf Oil decoration (orange and light blue). Based on the car that won the 1970 World Grand Prix Championship. Teamed with Ferrari 512M (1763) in Grand Prix sets. Klein-sculpted body.

1758 1971 Plymouth 'Cuda funny car (1971–74), 59

5784, 5790 (SC)

blue/white	$70
bright orange/yellow/purple	$45
white/blue/red stripes	$35
white/mustard/orange stripes	$30
white/mustard/red	$30
white/orange	$30
white/red	$30
white/red/medium blue	$40
white/red/yellow	$30
white/yellow/orange	$40

Keeler wanted a line of funny car dragsters and asked Ratkiewich to design this, the first in the series.

1759 1971 Vega Van "Gasser" (1971–74), 59

5781, 5782, 5783 (SC)

mustard/red flames	$25
bright orange/red flames	$25
white/fluorescent red-orange flames	$55
white/red flames	$25
bright yellow/red flames	$25

Ratkiewich-designed body.

1760 1957 Chevy Nomad (1971–74), 59

1903 (MT)

medium blue	$30
translucent blue	$35
medium blue/silver stripes	$80
brown	$150
lime green	$70
lime green/dark green stripes	$70
lime green/silver stripes	$90
bright orange	$30
bright orange/light orange stripes	$80
pink	$55
pink/cranberry stripe	$100
bright orange/blue exhausts	$55

bright orange/white exhausts $55
lemon yellow/orange exhausts $55
Ratkiewich wanted a 1955, but Keeler chose 1957. Ratkiewich-designed body. Classic design and wild colors made it one of Aurora's best-selling cars.

1761 Pinto funny car (1972–74), 61
5785, 5789 (SC)
lime green/medium blue/silver $45
lime green/green/silver $25
translucent green/green/silver $25
bright orange/purple/silver $25
white/blue/silver $25
Ratkiewich-designed body.

1762 Plymouth Road Runner stock car (1972–74), 61
1904 (MT)
bright blue/red #43 $45
medium blue/white #43 $75
red #43 $100
red/blue #43 $55
red/white #43 $100
white/blue #43 $25
yellow #43 $75
yellow/orange #43 $20
Number 43 is Richard Petty's car, although Aurora didn't explicitly market the car as such. An unlicensed product during a time when few bothered with license agreements. Ratkiewich-designed body.

1763 Ferrari 512 M (1972–74), 61
1799 (AFT), 1905 (MT), 1974 (AFT)
ultramarine blue/yellow #6 $30
red/white/silver #2 $25
white/silver $25
Teamed with Porsche 917 (1757) in Grand Prix sets. Klein-sculpted body.

1764 Javelin Trans-Am (1972–74), 61
1906 (MT)
blue/black black #5 $30
blue/black silver #5 $20
mustard/black/red black #5 $40
mustard/black/red silver #5 $30
red/white #5 $30
red/white/ultramarine blue #6 $40
Mark Donahue won the Trans-Am series in the red/white/ultramarine blue version of this car. Sears sponsored the AMC race team; Aurora built this car to please one of its largest customers, Sears. Ratkiewich-designed body.

1765 Javelin pro stocker (1972–74), 61
lime green/black $65
orange/black $50
white/purple $110
bright yellow/black $40
Same body as 1764 with air scoop on hood.

1766 Corvette funny car (1972–74), 61
5786 (SC)
bright orange/purple $40
white/red/medium blue $35
bright yellow/black $35
Ratkiewich-designed body.

1767 Lola T-260 Can-Am (1972–74), 60
1907 (MT), 3008 (U5)
white/red/black #1 $15
L & M logo. Klein-sculpted body.

1768 Shadow Can-Am (1972–74), 60
1908 (MT), 3007 (U5)
black #101 $15
Shadow logo on spoiler, UOP on fender. Model of car sponsored by Universal Oil Products and driven by Jackie Oliver in the 1971 Can-Am season. Klein-sculpted body.

1769 Ford "Baja Bronco" (1972–74), 60
1909 (MT)
medium blue/black/white/chrome #3 $35
mustard/black/white/chrome #3 $60
red/black/white/chrome #3 $25
yellow/black/white/chrome #3 $25
translucent yellow/black/white/chrome #3 $25
Ratkiewich-designed and Klein-sculpted body.

1773 Dodge Charger stock car (1972–74), 60
1910 (MT)
lime green/black blue #11 $45
lime green/black red #11 $45
white/black red #11 $25
mustard/black red #11 $20
Ratkiewich-designed body.

1775 Bre-Datsun 240Z (1973–74), 60
1911 (MT)
red/white #46 $20
Initially available at Datsun dealers with special decals. Klein drove a real one and sculpted the HO body.

1776 Bre-Datsun 510 Trans-Am (1973–74), 60

1912 (MT)

blue/white #35	$25
red/white #35	$20
red/white #46	$25
turquoise/white #35	$40

Available initially at Datsun dealers with special decals. Aurora received permission from the Sports Car Club of America to use the "Trans-Am" race series trademark. Klein-sculpted body. Aurora R&D team member Bernhard raced one of the real cars.

1777 1955 Chevy Bel Air (1973–74), 60

1913 (MT)

bright blue	$30
lime green	$45
orange	$30
red-orange	$30
bright yellow/white headers/ red	$35

Ratkiewich-designed body; he regretted chrome strip on sides had to be broken because of overscale front wheel well. The red-orange re-creates original Chevy color.

1778 VW "Baja Bug" (1973–74), 60

1914 (MT)

green/blue	$30
lime green/blue	$30
translucent green/blue	$30
orange/black	$25
red-orange/black	$30
red/black	$30
red/white	$25
white/black	$50
cream/black	$60
snow white/black	$50
bright yellow/black	$30
translucent yellow/black	$35

Klein-sculpted body.

1781 Roarin' Rolls "Golden Ghost" (1973–74), 63

1923 (MT)

black/white	$20
white/black	$25
bright yellow/black	$20
translucent yellow/black	$20

"Specialty Car" on a chassis ¼" longer than regular AFX chassis, with a narrow rear end to accommodate wide slicks and smaller front wheels. Four-gear (vs. five) drive train. Body mounted to one post, unlike regular clip-on bodies. Gold chrome. Twin drag chutes. Winged ghost hood ornament. Ratkiewich-designed body.

1782 Peace Tank (1973–74), 63

1924 (MT)

olive green	$20
translucent green	$20

"Specialty Car" on same chassis as 1781 Roarin' Rolls. Model has Chrysler Hemi engine. Turret swivels. Push down canon barrel and driver head pops up. Knot in cannon barrel reflects anti-Vietnam sentiment within Aurora's R&D team. Guitar on hood, beer can on rear. Driver inspired by Aurora president Diker. Vernon-designed body.

1786 Porsche 510K Can-Am (1973–74), 63

1915 (MT), 3002 (U5)

blue/yellow/red white #6 SUNOCO	$35
blue/yellow/red white #7 SUNOCO	$35
red/yellow/white #4 SUNOCO	$35
red/yellow/white #6	$30
white/red/black #6	$25
white/red/black #6 L & M	$25

Porsche-Audi sticker on side. Available first at Sears Christmas 1972 with special sticker. Spoiler tilts. Klein-carved body.

1787 Matador stock car (1973–74), 63

1916 (MT)

red/white/ultramarine blue #16	$45
white/blue #2	$25
yellow/red #2	$35

Available first at Sears Christmas 1972. Modeled on Mark Donahue's car as sponsored by Sears. Ratkiewich-designed body.

1791 '31 Model A Ford panel (1973–74), 63

1925 (MT)

bright blue/black	$35
lime green/black	$25
translucent green/black	$30
mustard/black	$25
orange/black	$55

"Specialty Car" on same chassis as 1781 Roarin' Rolls. Different version of 1746, 1928. Vernon-designed body.

AFX FLAMETHROWERS

1798 Flamethrower Porsche 917 (1972–74), 63

1757 (AFX), 1902 (MT), 1973 (MTF)

light blue/orange #2	$25
white/purple	$20
yellow/blue	$15

1799 Flamethrower Ferrari 512 M (1972–74), 63
1763 (AFX), 1905(MT), 1974 (MTF)
ultramarine blue/yellow #6 $30
red/white/silver #6 $25

1973 Magna-Traction Flamethrower Porsche 917 (1975–77), 67
1902 (MT), 1757 (AFX), 1798 (AFT)
light blue/orange #2 $25
white/green #2 $20
bright yellow/blue #2 $15

1974 Magna-Traction Flamethrower Ferrari 512 M (1975–77), 67
1905 (MT), 1763 (AFX), 1799 (AFT)
bright blue/white/silver #2 $20
red/white/silver #6 $30
white/blue/silver #2 $20

1975 Magna-Traction Flamethrower Chevelle stocker (1977), 67
1929 (MT)
orange/white/black #17 $35
white/orange/silver #17 $25
bright yellow/red/black #17 $20

1976 Magna-Traction Flamethrower Charger Daytona (1977), 67
1753 (AFX), 1900 (MT)
blue/black #7 $35
yellow/black #7 $30
opaque yellow/black #7 $30

DRAGSTERS

Aurora used the "specialty" chassis to accommodate wide slicks and an extension to produce a dragster chassis. Six-gear drive train, not the usual five. They were first issued with AFX motors, later with Magna-Traction motors. Came in a domed package with decal sheet. Richard Ratkiewich and John Vernon designed the bodies.

1772 Dodge Fever (AFX) (1973–74), 65
1961 (Magna-Traction) 75–76
white/fogged yellow $35
Same body as 1792. Ratkiewich-designed body.

1774 Furious Fueler (AFX) (1973–74), 65
1962 (Magna-Traction) 75–76
white/fogged yellow $35
Same body as 1794. Vernon-designed body.

1792 Aztec (AFX) (1973–74), 65
1963 (Magna-Traction) 75–76
red metallic $55
Same body as 1772. Ratkiewich-designed body.

1794 Dyno-Mite (AFX) (1973–74), 65
1964 (Magna-Traction) 75–76
white/fogged blue $55
Same body as 1774. Vernon-designed body.

AFX MAGNA-TRACTION

In 1975 the AFX chassis was modified to lower the motor magnets close to the metal power strips in Aurora track. Magnetic attraction would thus hold the cars to the track during operation. Magnets show through the chassis bottom. Most existing AFX car bodies were modified to fit the new chassis; all subsequent new cars featured Magna-Traction.

1900 Dodge Charger Daytona (1975–77)
1753 (AFX), 1976 (MTF)
blue/black #7 $35
greenish-blue/black #7 $35
orange/black #7 $40
yellow/black #7 $35
translucent yellow/black #7 $35

1901 Camaro Z-28 (1975–77)
1756 (AFX)
light blue/purple #3 $25
white/blue/red/silver #6 $25

1902 Porsche 917 (1975–77) $15
1757 (AFX), 1798 (AFT), 1973 (MTF)
light blue/orange #2 $25
white/green/yellow #2 $20
yellow/blue #2

1903 1957 Chevy Nomad (1975–77)
1760 (AFX)
blue $30
greenish-blue $30
orange $40
orange/yellow stripes $80
pink $55
pink/cranberry stripes $100
red/white stripes $85

1904 Plymouth Road Runner (1975–77)
1762 (AFX)
bright blue red #43 $45

medium blue white #43	$75
red white #43	$100
red blue #43	$50
white black #43	$115
white blue #43	$20
yellow white #43	$20
yellow orange #43	$20

1905 Ferrari 512 M (1975–77)

1763 (AFX), 1799 (AFT), 1974 (MTF)

blue/silver	$20
blue/white/silver #2	$20
blue/white/silver #6	$20
red/silver	$20
red/white/silver #2	$20
red/white/silver #6	$30
white/silver	$20
white/blue/silver #2	$20
white/blue/silver #6	$20

1906 Javelin AMX Trans-Am (1975–77)

1764 (AFX)

blue/black black #5	$30
blue/black silver #5	$20
mustard/black/red black #5	$40
mustard/black/red/silver #5	$30
red/white/blue #6	$35

1907 Lola T-260 Can-Am (1975–77)

1767 (AFX), 3008 (U5)

white/red/black #1 L & M	$20

1908 Shadow Can-Am (1975–77)

1768 (AFX), 3007 (U5)

black/white #101 Shadow	$15

1909 Ford "Baja Bronco" (1975–77)

1769 (AFX)

medium blue/black/white/ chrome #3	$35
mustard/black/white/ chrome #3	$60
red/black/white/chrome #3	$25
yellow/black/white/ chrome #3	$20
translucent yellow/black/ white/chrome #3	$25

1910 Dodge Charger stock car (1975–77)

1773 (AFX)

mustard/black #11	$20
orange/black #11	$40
white/black #11	$25
bright yellow/black #11	$20

1911 Bre-Datsun 240Z (1975–77)

1775 (AFX)

white/lime green #46	$20
white/red #46	$20

1912 Bre-Datsun 510 Trans-Am (1975–77)

1776 (AFX)

blue/white #35	$30
red/white #35	$25
yellow/orange #46	$20

1913 1955 Chevy Bel Air (1975–77)

1777 (AFX)

bright blue	$30
lime green	$50
red-orange	$30
bright yellow	$25

1914 "Baja Bug" VW (1975–77)

1778 (AFX)

green/blue	$30
lime green/blue	$30
orange/black	$30
red-orange/black	$30
red/black	$30
red/white	$30
white/black	$50
cream/black	$60
snow white/black	$50
yellow/black	$30
translucent yellow/black	$35

1915 Porsche 510K Can-Am (1975–77)

1786 (AFX), 3002 (U5)

blue/yellow/red white SUNOCO #6	$35
blue/yellow/red white SUNOCO #7	$35
orange/yellow/white SUNOCO #4	$40
red/yellow/white #6	$25
white/green SUNOCO #5	$55
white/red/black #6	$25
white/red/black #6 L & M	$25
white/red/black SUNOCO #6	$45
yellow/blue SUNOCO #2	$45

Porsche-Audi on side.

1916 AMC Matador stock car (1975)
1787 (AFX), 1938 (Police), 1939 (Taxi)
red/white/blue #16 $45
white/blue #2 $30
yellow/red #2 $35

1919 Datsun Baja pickup (1975–77)
1745 (AFX)
blue/black #211 $20
mustard/black #211 $20
lemon yellow/black #211 $20

1920 1929 Model A Woody (1975–77)
1746 (AFX)
black/wood $20

1921 Porsche 917-10 Can-Am (1975–77)
1747 (AFX), 3001 (U5)
white/blue/red #16 $15
white/blue/red #23 $60
RC Cola logo on nose and spoiler.

1922 Dodge Street Van (1975–77)
1748 (AFX)
lime green/blue $20
opaque green/blue $30
orange $15
orange/black $10
bright yellow/orange $15

1923 Roarin' Rolls "Golden Ghost" (1975–77)
1781 (AFX)
black/white $20
white/black $25
bright yellow/black $20
translucent yellow/black $30

1924 Peace Tank (1975–77)
1782 (AFX)
olive green $15
opaque green $15

1925 1931 Model A Ford panel (1975–77)
1791 (AFX)
lime green/black $25
opaque green/black $25
mustard/black $25
yellow/black $25

1926 Grand Am (1975–77)
1702 (AFX)
ultramarine blue/yellow/red $75
white/red/blue $25
yellow/orange $25

1927 Corvette (1975–77)
1703 (AFX)
black/yellow $50
medium blue/white $50
chrome/light blue $30
chrome/red $25
white/blue/red/no stripes #7 $40
white/blue/red/no stripes/ silver lights, gas cap #7 $40
white/blue/red/silver stripes #7 $25
bright yellow/black $25
The #7 car was inspired by the American flag and issued for the 1976 Bicentennial. Ratkiewich-designed body.

1928 Model A 1930 Ford coupe (1975–77), 69
black/black $35
bright blue/black $35
greenish blue/black $30
bright yellow/black $25
"Specialty" chassis. Different version of 1746, 1791. Vernon-designed body.

1929 Chevelle stocker (1975–77), 69
1975 (MTF)
blue/lime green #17 $140
white/orange/silver #17 $30
bright yellow/red/black #17 $30
427 on hood. Ratkiewich-designed body.

1930 AMC Matador stock car (1975–77), 69
3005 (U5)
orange/black/red/silver #5, 425 on hood $25
white/blue/red/silver #5 $25
Mark Donahue won Riverside in this car. Aurora built AMC cars because favored customer Sears sponsored the real race cars. Hill-designed body.

1931 VW Thing (1975–77), 69
Canvas top version of 1936.
blue/white $15
yellow/black $15
Vernon- and Ratkiewich-designed, Klein-carved body.

1932 Mercury stocker (1976–77), 69
3006 (U5)
light blue/white/dark blue #31 $25
white/black/gold #31 $25
"429CI" on hood. Modeled on the Woods Brothers stock car. Hill-designed body.

1933 Porsche Carrera (1976–77), 69
orange/blue/black #3 $20
white/black/burgundy #3 $20
Modeled on one of the set of matched Porsches used in the International Race of Champions. Hill-designed body. Vernon described the body as a "fat guppy," which challenged Aurora designers to devise paint schemes to make it look thinner.

1934 Vega funny car (1976–77), 69, 70
orange/white/red $20
white/orange/blue/silver $30
Body created by an independent design shop in Philadelphia.

1935 Capri funny car (1976–77), 70
blue/black/white #13 $30
blue/black/white #13 no #13 on hood $35
orange/white/maroon #13 $30
orange/white/maroon #13 no #13 on hood $35
white/green/blue #21 $25
Hill-designed body. In reality, a rally car.

1936 VW Thing roadster (1976–77), 70
Open top version of 1931.
brown camouflage $25
green camouflage $25
R&D team member Bernhard explains the camouflage: "Boredom had struck the R&D department!"

1937 Dodge Van rescue vehicle (1976–77), 70
Ambulance version of 1922.
red/white/gold $20
white/orange/red $20
"Rescue" on sides. Hill-designed top.

1938 Matador police car (1977), 70
1916 (stock version), 1939 (taxi)
blue/white/black $30
white/black $25

1939 Matador taxi (1977), 70
1916 (stock), 1938 (police)
light blue $30
white $15
yellow $20

1941 1956 Ford pickup (1977), 70
black/red & white flames $45
black/yellow & red flames $45
red/white & blue flames $45

1942 Custom Van (1977), 70
orange/red $20
orange/violet $20
white/blue $20

G-PLUS

Late 1975 saw the introduction of a series of new cars with an in-line motor—a total departure for Aurora. The in-line armature and magnets are visible from the underside of the chassis. The earliest cars have Mabuchi motors, the rest feature Singapore-made Aurora motors. Bodies snap onto ears on chassis sides. All bodies were sculpted by Ron Klein.

1731 Lola T-330 (1976–77), 72
white/blue/orange/chrome #7 $35
white/blue/light blue/red/chrome #7 $30
yellow/red/chrome #7 $30
"Lola 7" on spoiler.

1732 Ferrari 312 PB (1976–77), 72
red/yellow/silver #2 $25
red/white/silver #2 $25

1733 McLaren F-1 (1976–77), 72
white/orange #11 $25
white/orange #11 without air scoop $50
white/red/black #11 $25
Texaco/Marlboro logos. The white/red version is the 1974 World Grand Prix Championship McLaren of Emerson Fittipaldi; white/orange is that of world champion James Hunt.

1734 Ferrari F-1 (1976–77), 72
red/white/black #6 $35
Goodyear logo. Paired with the McLaren F-1 (1733) in the *Monaco Grand Prix race set (2108). Represents Niki Lauda's Ferrari 312T.*

1735 Indy Special (1976–77), 72

black/red-orange/yellow/ white #1	$20
white/red-orange-yellow #1	$40

Goodyear logo.

1736 Ferrari Daytona coupe (1976–77), 72

yellow/green/black #16	$25
yellow/lime green/black #16	$25

1737 Rallye Ford Escort (1977), 72

green/yellow/blue #28	$25

XLERATORS AND XLERATORS II

XLerators were the first slotless race cars. They appeared in 1973 with AFX motors and were first offered exclusively by Montgomery Ward. Improvements led to XLerators II with G-Plus, first marketed in 1976. When XLerators II replaced first issues, catalog numbers changed; new numbers are indicated after the slash. Since the bodies were old Thunderjets, they attach by screw posts front and rear.

2741 Ferrari GTO 250 (1973), 64

1368 (Thunderjet 500 version), 1493 (FT)

red/white #1	$50

2742 Ford GT (1973), 64

1374 (Thunderjet 500 version), 1395 (CC), 1417 (WO), 1472 (TO), 1494 (FT)

blue/black #2	$50

2741 Camaro (1974–75), 64

1388 (Thunderjet 500 version), 1418 (WO), 1480 (TO)

orange/white #1	$35
red/white #1	$35
white/blue #1	$35

2742/2788 Pontiac Firebird hardtop (1974–77), 64

1402 (Thunderjet 500 version), 1478 (TO)

blue/black-silver #2	$45
blue/red & yellow firebird/#2	$40
yellow/black-silver #2	$40

2743/2783 Ford "J" (1973–77), 64

1382 (Thunderjet 500 version), 1430 (FT)

bright orange/black/silver #3	$15
red/yellow/white #3	$20
yellow/black/silver #3	$20
translucent yellow/black/silver	$25

2744/2748 Chaparral 2F (1973–77), 64

1410 (Thunderjet 500 version), 1476 (TO), 1491 (FT)

lime green/black/silver #4	$30
translucent green/black/ silver #4	$30
mustard/black/silver #4	$30
orange/black/silver	$30
white/blue #4	$25
white/lime green #4	$20

2746 Chevy pro-stock Vega (1974–75), 64

orange/black/red #3	$65
white/black/green #3	$85

Body original with Xlerators.

2747/2785 Chevy Baja Blazer (1974–76), 64

orange/blue/white #4	$25
white/blue/red #4	$45
white/blue/black #4	$30
white/black/red #4	$30
yellow/black/orange #4	$30

Body original with Xlerators.

2781/2786 Mercury Cougar hardtop (1975–77), 64

1389 (Thunderjet 500 version), 1419 (WO), 1479 (TO)

mustard/blue/white #3	$35
white/blue/red #3	$40
white/black/red #3	$45

2782/2787 Willys "Gasser" (1975–77), 64

1401 (Thunderjet 500 version), 1474 (TO)

red/black/yellow #4	$50
white/black/blue #4	$70
yellow/black/green #4	$35

ULTRA 5

This Aurora slotless race set was introduced in 1977. Cars were designated "A" or "B" depending on which power rails they ran.

3001 Porsche 917-10 Can-Am "A" (1977)

1747 (AFX), 1921 (MT)

white/yellow-blue-green #11	$25
white/yellow-blue-green #11 AURORA	$25

3002 Porsche 510K Can-Am "B" (1977)

1786 (AFX), 1915 (MT)

light blue/yellow/purple #6	$30
white/yellow/blue/red #6 AUTOWORLD	$20

3005 Matador stocker "A" (1977)
1930 (MT)
white/yellow/red #1 $25

3006 Mercury stocker "B" (1977)
1932 (MT)
white/red/blue #2 $25

3007 Shadow Can-Am "A" (1977)
1768 (AFX), 1908 (MT)
black/orange-yellow-white #3 $30
white/red-orange-yellow #3 $25
white/red-orange-yellow #3 GOODYEAR $25

3008 Lola T260 Can-Am "B" (1977)
1767 (AFX), 1907 (MT)
white/blue-green-yellow #39 $15
white/blue-green-yellow #39 LOLA $20

SCREECHERS

Screechers were first sold in 1976 as a preassembled, battery-powered slotless set for young children. In 1977 car catalog numbers were changed; new numbers follow the slash.

Screechers sets

5755 Firemen's Thrill Show (1977)
26" x 17" base $60–$100

5756 Interstate Chase (1977)
33" x 22" base $70–$100

5757 Spider-Man Meets the Fly (1977)
33" x 22" base $80–$110

5758 Drag City (1977)
41" x 30" base $70–$100

Screechers Cars

5781/5801 Smokies Magnum Wagon police car (1976–77)
1759 (AFX), 5782, 5783 (SC)
white/black $15
Star of the Interstate Chase set 5756.

5782/5802 Rapid Rescue (1976–77)
1759 (AFX), 5781, 5783 (SC)
yellow/red "Rescue 1" $15

5783/5803 Super Chief (1976–77)
1759 (AFX), 5781, 578 (SC)
white/red flames $15
Star of the Fireman's Thrill Show set 5755.

5784/5804 Flaming 'Cuda (1976–77)
1758 (AFX), 5790 (SC)
white/red & tan flames $20
white/flames on top & sides $35

5785/5805 Pinto Thunderbolt (1976–77)
1761 (AFX), 5789 (SC)
light blue/dark blue/white $15

5786/5806 "76" Supervette (1976–77)
1766 (AFX)
white/red/blue stars #76 $20
off-white/red/blue stars #76 $20
white/black stars $15
Bicentennial commemorative.

5787/5807 Terrible Turbo (1976–77)
1755 (AFX), 5811 (SC)
blue/red/white #7 $15

5788/5808 Double Trouble (1976–77)
1754 (AFX), 5812 (SC)
lime green/blue $15
yellow/orange #5 $15

5789/5809 Potent Pinto (1976–77)
1761 (AFX), 5785 (AFX)
orange/blue #22 $20

5790/5810 Super Cuda (1976–77)
1758 (AFX), 5784 (SC)
orange/yellow/red $15

5811 Spider Mobile (1977), 72
1755 (AFX), 5787 (SC)
blue/red/white web $50
Star of Spider-Man Meets the Fly set 5757.

5812 Fly Mobile (1977), 72
1754 (AFX), 5788 (SC)
green/black fly paint $30

ROAD BURNERS

This 1977-only set was marketed as a battery-powered toy race set for younger children. Track was regular AFX issue. Cars have AFX bodies with air foils removed. Chassis and motor are from the G-Plus line with weaker magnets. Perhaps as few as 5,000 sets sold.

2001 Ferrari 612 Can-Am
1751 (AFX)
orange $20
red $20

2002 Auto World McLaren XLR Can-Am
1752 (AFX)
orange $20
red $20

CIGARBOX CARS

Cigarbox Cars went on the market in 1968 and were superseded by Speedline later that same year. Chassis is die-cast metal with Aurora logo, name of car, and catalog number imprinted on the bottom. Wheels are T-jet. All of the bodies are T-jet, except for the Formula I racers specially created for this series. It is not certain if all cars listed were actually issued.

Collectors are beginning to take these cars seriously. Only a few colors are known and more colors are sure to surface. Mint cars in the box sell in the $20–$25 range; loose mint cars, $10–$15.

Speedline bodies fit on Thunderjet chassis; collectors must be certain a body represented as a Thunderjet body is genuine and not a Cigarbox body. To tell the difference, look for small variations in the height of the screw posts—compare the unknown body to a genuine T-jet.

53 Ice Cream truck (1972), 44
white $60
Good Humor promotional item.

6101 Stingray (1968)
1356 (Thunderjet 500 version), 6801 (SL)
off-white $20–$25

6102 Ferrari Berlinetta
1368 (Thunderjet 500 version), 6802 (SL)
tan/black $20–$25
off-white/red $20–$25

6103 Mako Shark
1380 (Thunderjet 500 version), 6803 (SL)
red $20–$25

6104 Ford "J"
1382 (Thunderjet 500 version), 6804 (SL)
gray $20–$25
red/black $20–$25

6105 Ford GT
1374 (Thunderjet 500 version), 6805 (SL)
turquoise/black $20–$25
off-white/black $20–$25
yellow/black $20–$25

6106 Lola GT
1378 (Thunderjet 500 version), 6806 (SL)
turquoise/black $20–$25
off-white/red $20–$25
green/white $20–$25

6107 Ford XL 500
1386 (Thunderjet 500 version), 6807 (SL)
off-white/turquoise $20–$25
dark green $20–$25

6108 Toronado
1379 (Thunderjet 500 version)
turquoise $20–$25

6109 Riviera
1357 (Thunderjet 500 version), 6809 (SL)
turquoise $20–$25
off-white $20–$25

6110 Thunderbird
1383 (Thunderjet 500 version), 6810 (SL)
off-white $20–$25
yellow $20–$25

6111 Dino Ferrari
1381 (Thunderjet 500 version), 6811 (SL)
red/white $20–$25
tan $20–$25
turquoise/black $20–$25
yellow/red $20–$25

6112 Porsche 904
1376 (Thunderjet 500 version), 6812 (SL)
chrome silver/black $20–$25
red/white $20–$25
turquoise/black $20–$25
white/red $20–$25
yellow $20–$25
This is actually a Porsche 906, and is correctly identified in the Thunderjet 500 series.

6113 Cobra
1375 (Thunderjet 500 version), 6813 (SL)
green/white $20–$25
tan/black $20–$25
turquoise/black $20–$25

6114 Chaparral
1377 (Thunderjet 500 version)
red/white #5 $20–$25
tan #3 $20–$25
tan #7 $20–$25
turquoise #5 $20–$25
turquoise #7 $20–$25
white #2 $20–$25
off-white/black #2 $20–$25
off-white/black #7 $20–$25

6115 Camaro
1388 (Thunderjet 500 version), 6815 (SL) $20–$25

6116 Cougar
1389 (Thunderjet 500 version), 6816 (SL) $20–$25

6117 McLaren Elva
1397 (Thunderjet 500 version)
white/red $20–$25
peach chrome $20–$25

6118 Mustang convertible
1371 (Thunderjet 500 version), 6818 (SL)
green $20–$25

6119 Dune Buggy $20–$25

6120 Mangusta
1400 (Thunderjet 500 version), 6820 (SL) $20–$25

6121 Lola Ford Formula I
candy lavender $20–$25
Yanchus-sculpted body.

6122 Ferrari Formula I
lavender $20–$25
Ron Kohn sculpted body.

6123 Cooper Maserati Formula I
gold $20–$25
Yanchus- and Brand-sculpted body.

6124 Lotus Ford Formula I
lavender $20–$25
Kohn- and Yanchus-sculpted body.

6125 Honda Formula I
candy orange $20–$25
Kohn-sculpted body.

6126 BRM Formula I
candy lavender $20–$25
candy orange $20–$25
copper $20–$25
Kohn-sculpted body.

6127 Jaguar XKE $20–$25

6128 1965 Ford Mustang hardtop
$20–$25

6129 AC Cobra $20–$25

6130 Pontiac Firebird
light candy red $20–$25

6131 Willys "Gasser"
black $100
mustard $40
pink $125
purple $80
tan $20

6132 Hot Rod $20–$25

6133 Cheetah $20–$25

SPEEDLINE

Speedline cars replaced Cigar Box in the fall of 1968. Bodies have brighter metallic paint. Chassis are still Cigarbox—they even say Cigarbox—but wheels are hard plastic. Speedline cars still sold in 1969 and some were reissued in 1973. Most 1973 reissues are unpainted plastic and lack clear windows. Paper sticker on 1973 issues says "Made in Singapore." Mint cars on blistercards sell in the $20–$30 range.

6801 Stingray
1356 (Thunderjet 500 version), 6101 (CB)
purple chrome $20–$30

6802 Ferrari Berlinetta
1368 (Thunderjet 500 version), 6102 (CB)
candy light red/silver $20–$30
candy red/silver $20–$30

6803 Mako Shark
1380 (Thunderjet 500 version), 6103 (CB)
$20–$30

6804 Ford J
1382 (Thunderjet 500 version), 6104 (CB)
yellow $20–$30

6805 Ford GT
1374 (Thunderjet 500 version), 6105 (CB)
purple chrome $20–$30
lemon 73 issue $20–$30

6806 Lola GT
1378 (Thunderjet 500 version), 6106 (CB)
gold/silver $20–$30

6807 Ford XL 500
1386 (Thunderjet 500 version), 6107 (CB)
candy lavender/silver $20–$30
gold/silver $20–$30
light blue $20–$30

6809 Riviera
1357 (Thunderjet 500 version), 6109 (CB)
dark candy red/silver $20–$30
light candy red/silver $20–$30

6810 Thunderbird
1383 (Thunderjet 500 version), 6110 (CB)
candy gold/silver $20–$30

6811 Dino Ferrari
1381 (Thunderjet 500 version), 6111 (CB)
blue 73 issue $20–$30
mustard 73 issue $20–$30

6812 Porsche 904
1376 (Thunderjet 500 version), 6112 (CB)
lavender chrome $20–$30
This is actually a Porsche 906.

6813 Cobra GT
1375 (Thunderjet 500 version), 6113 (CB)
purple chrome/silver $20–$30

6814 Chaparral
1377 (Thunderjet 500 version), 6114 (CB)
off-white 73 issue $20–$30

6815 Camaro
1388 (Thunderjet 500 version), 6115 (CB)

6816 Cougar
1389 (Thunderjet 500 version), 6116 (CB)
candy gold/silver $20–$30

6818 Mustang convertible
1371 (Thunderjet 500 version), 6118 (CB)
$20–$30

6820 Mangusta
1400 (Thunderjet 500 version), 6120 (CB)
chrome $20–$30

6827 XKE Jaguar
1358 (Thunderjet 500 version)
chrome red $20–$30

6828 Mustang hardtop
1372 (Thunderjet 500 version)
$20–$30

6829 AC Cobra
1370 (Thunderjet 500 version)
candy lavender/silver $20–$30

6830 Firebird
1402 (Thunderjet 500 version)
$20–$30

6831 Willys "Gasser"
1401 (Thunderjet 500 version)
purple chrome/silver $20–$30

6833 Cheetah
1403 (Thunderjet 500 version)
copper/silver $20–$30

6853 Volkswagen
1404 (Thunderjet 500 version)
gold chrome $20–$30

6821 Lola Ford Formula I
$20–$30

6822 Ferrari Formula I $20–$30

6823 Cooper Maserati Formula I
$20–$30

6824 Lotus Ford Formula I
$20–$30

6825 Honda Formula I $20–$30

6826 BRM Formula I $20–$30

6854 Dodge Charger $20–$30

6855 Ford Torino
1408 (Thunderjet 500 version)
white (painted) 73 issue $20–$30

6856 Alfa Romeo $20–$30

SUPER SPEEDSTERS

A few of the Speedline cars reappeared in 1975. Cars were manufactured in the Orient and blistercarded in the United States. Chassis is Cigarbox. Most cars lack clear windows. A blistercarded set of three cars sells in the $30–40 range.

Pontiac Firebird
1402 (Thunderjet 500 version)
copper-plated

Willys "Gasser"
1401 (Thunderjet 500 version)
blue

Lola GT
1378 (Thunderjet 500 version)
black
blue
red
Molded with a hole in the center of the roof so the car would whistle as it sped down a track.

Ford J
1382 (Thunderjet 500 version)
blue

FLASHBACK

In 1969 Aurora sold a playset that involved sending two cars racing back and forth on a drag strip of orange track. Propulsion came from two squeeze bulbs that pushed the cars out of the grandstand, down the track, into a large rubber band in the pit station, and back up the track to the grandstand. The cars had extra-large wheels, and thus the wheel wells were cut out to an extra depth. Chassis is Cigarbox.

6103 Mako Shark
1380 (Thunderjet 500 version)
metallic orange/silver stripe $20

6108 Toronado
1379 (Thunderjet 500 version)
metallic purple/silver stripe $20

HO STRUCTURES

Aurora began manufacturing HO buildings for model railroad layouts in the late 1950s. When Model Motoring arrived, Aurora issued six injection-molded plastic kits for slot car raceways.

658 Service station (1961–62)
$110
"Model Motoring Service Center." White/red/gray/clear plastic. Garage bay doors open. Decals for Texaco or Aurora signs. Designed to work with both HO model railroad and slot car layouts, the synergy did not work and the kit was discontinued after two years.

1450 Start-finish pylons (1963–73)
$20
White plastic. Spring-loaded flags flip up when hay bale is pressed.

1451 Judges stand (1963–73)
$25
Gray plastic. Paper flag sheet included.

1452 Grandstand (1963–73)
$25
Brown/gray plastic. Includes TV cameras and "Aurora Model Motoring Grandstand" decal.

1453 Double station pit stop (1963–73)
$50
Beige/gray plastic. "Corvette" and "Thunderbird" sign decals.

1456 Curved bleachers (1963–73)
$25
Dark brown plastic. Decal sheet with real-life advertisements; paper pennant sheet. Curve fits the radius of Aurora's 9" curved track section.

1498 Start-finish pylons and judges stand (1974–77)
$35
Repackage of 1450, 1451.

1499 Grandstand, dual pit stop, curved bleachers (1974–77) $60
Repackage of 1452, 1453, 1456.

SUPER MODEL MOTORING

Issued at the height of the slot car boom, these 1/48 scale cars were intended to find a niche between HO cars and 1/32 scale. They are powered by regular T-jet motors. Hot rod-style bodies were all produced by HMS.

1751 1931 Ford Hot-Rod pickup (1964–65), 27

gray/black	$75
red/black	$60
tan/black	$45
turquoise/black	$45
white/black	$45
yellow/black	$45

1752 1932 Ford chopped sedan (1964–65), 27

gray	$70
red	$55
tan	$55
turquoise	$55
white	$55
yellow	$55

1753 1936 Ford convertible coupe (1964–65), 27

gray	$70
red	$55
tan	$55
turquoise	$55
white	$55
yellow	$55

1754 1957 Chevrolet coupe (1964–65), 27

gray	$60
red	$55
tan	$55
turquoise	$55
white	$55
yellow	$55

1755 1949 Mercury Hot Rod coupe (1964–65), 27

gray	$60
red	$55
tan	$55
turquoise	$55
white	$55
yellow	$55

1756 1957 Thunderbird Hot Rod coupe (1964–65), 27

gray	$80
red	$65
tan	$65
turquoise	$60
white	$60
yellow	$60

1757 1927 Ford T Hot Rod (1964–65), 27

gray	$85
red/tan	$65
tan/brown	$65
white/green	$85
white/red	$60
yellow/brown	$60
yellow/green	$60

1758 1932 Ford Deuce Hot Rod (1964–65)

gray	$75
red	$75

tan $65
turquoise $65
white $75
yellow $65

AURORA 1/32 CARS

Between 1965 and 1967 Aurora issued ten cars in the Aurora Americans A-Jet series. The bodies were the same as Aurora's static model kits and K&B nos. 1825–1833. Unlike the K&B kits, Aurora's cars were ready-to-run. They had injection-molded bodies with chrome-plated and clear parts, A-Jet Sidewinder motors, aluminum frames, and rubber tires. Braided wire pickups were centered near the slot so cars would run on other track brands. Most had American flag stickers on their doors and wide racing stripes across their tops in a variety of colors, but some came without flags or stripes.

3251 Ford GT (1965–67), 34
white $60

3252 Pontiac GTO coupe (1965–67), 34
red $50
white $50
yellow $50
The GTO and Mustang were the most common bodies used in race sets.

3253 Mustang 350GT (1965–67), 34
red $40–$50
white $40–$50
yellow $40–$50
The Mustang and GTO were the most common bodies used in race sets. Aurora's original static kit is a stock Mustang fastback; this slot car version became a Shelby 350GT with the addition of a hood scoop.

3254 Corvair Corsa coupe (1965–67), 34
yellow $60

3255 Plymouth Barracuda (1965–67), 34
red $60

3256 Chaparral (1965–67), 34
white $50

3257 Cobra coupe (1965–67), 34
blue $55

3258 Comet Exterminator (1965–67), 34
red $60

3259 Lola T-70 (1966–67), 34
blue $60
Released a year after the initial eight cars.

3260 Rover BRM (1966–67)
dark metallic green $150
Extremely rare; it was released near the end of the A-Jet series.

The following four cars were listed in Aurora's 1966 and 1967 catalogs but apparently were never issued.

3261 Demolition Derby Buick
The prototype pattern was sculpted for this car.

3262 Demolition Derby Mercury
The prototype pattern was sculpted for this car.

3263 66 Oldsmobile Toronado

3264 Mako Shark
Aurora issued a static kit of this car.

3266 Thundercycle (1967), 39
red cycle/black rider $140
yellow cycle/black rider $140
Although sold to run on 1/32 track, the bike and rider are scaled at 1/24. Injection-molded body, chrome spoked wheels, Challenger motor, and aluminum frame. Two "training wheels" drive the cycle and keep it upright. Sold separately for $9.95 or in the Thundercycle Racing Set (3204). In the Groove (May 1967) noted that it ran more slowly than a car: "Wait till you check the handling. Good thing the poor guy is wearing leathers."

BIG CAR RACING

After a lapse of two years, Aurora revived 1/32 cars in 1970 with a home race set which included four cars and, in 1971, two tricycles. They have injection-molded bodies, plastic chassis, and in-line motor. Power pickups are metal shoes, and the power strips are positioned away from the slot. Clip-on braided pickups were included with each set so cars could be converted to run on conventional 1/32 track.

3351 Ferrari 612 (1970–71)

blue	$50
red	$50

Does not have real car's wing. Klein-sculpted body.

3352 McLaren M12 (1970–71)

orange	$50
white	$50

Does not have real car's wing. Klein-sculpted body.

3353 Mirage coupe (1970–71)

blue	$50
orange	$50

Klein-sculpted body.

3354 Ferrari 312P coupe (1970–71)

red	$50

Klein-sculpted body.

3357 Green Machine (1971), 39

black/metallic green.	$30

Three-wheel chopper cycle with "Crazy California styling." Designed to lift front wheel with acceleration. Sidewinder motor. Ratkiewich-designed body.

3358 Chopper Chariot (1971), 39

pink/purple	$30

Three-wheel cycle. Ratkiewich-designed body.

POWERSLICKS

Powerslicks came from Aurora's toy division. Battery-powered to run on their own special track. Plastic chassis attaches to the front and rear. Powerslicks have wide plastic front tires and rubber rear tires.

2151 Two-Much (1970–71)

black/metallic gold	$30
black/metallic red	$30

AFX version of this car body is 1754. HMS-created body.

2152 Turbo-Turnon (1970–71)

black/metallic green/metallic gold	$30

AFX version of this car body is 1755. HMS-created body.

2153 Mod Rod (1970–71)

black/metallic gold/metallic red	$50

Dodge Challenger; Innova-created body.

2154 Drag'n Devil (1970–71)

blue/red/white	$50

Open GT; Innova-created body.

2155 Bad Bandito (1970–71)

black/metallic copper/black	$50
black/metallic purple/silver	$50

Mustang; Innova-created body.

2156 Wild Winger (1970–71)

black/metallic blue/white/silver	$50

Ferrari; Innova-created body.

K&B 1/32 KITS

Aurora subsidiary K&B's boxed kits contain a blistercard with the injection-molded plastic car body, chrome-plated parts, clear plastic windows, Challenger Sidewinder motor, adjustable aluminum frame, aluminum wheels, rubber tires, and decal sheet with a selection of race numbers and stripes. They sold for $6. Bodies are from Aurora static kits and were also used for Aurora Americans A-Jets nos. 3251–3259. These 1/32 kits are harder to find today than K&B's larger scale kits.

1825 64 Ford GT coupe (1965–67)

white	$150

GT-40.

1826 65 Pontiac GTO coupe (1965–67)

dark blue	$150

1827 65 Mustang GT-350 (1965–67)

white, blue paint trim	$150

1828 65 Corvair Corsa coupe (1965–67)

light yellow	$150

1829 65 Plymouth Barracuda (1965–67)

dark red	$150

1830 64 Cobra Daytona coupe (1965–67)

blue	$150

1831 64 Chaparral 2 (1965–67)

white	$150

1832 65 Comet Exterminator coupe (1965–67)
red $150

1833 65 Ford Lola T-70 (1966–67), 35
blue $150
Car Model (September 1967): "K&B's Lola T-70 is more of a caricature than an accurate model of the real Lola's lines."

K&B INJECTION-MOLDED 1/32 CAR BODIES

Kits contained the same injection-molded plastic bodies, with clear and chrome plated plastic parts and a decal sheet. They sold for $1. Today they sell in the $35 range.

1825-1 64 Ford GT coupe
white $35
A GT-40.

1826-1 65 Pontiac GTO coupe
blue $35

1827-1 65 Mustang GT-350
white $35

1828-1 Corvair Corsa coupe
light yellow $35

1829-1 65 Plymouth Barracuda
red $35

1830-1 64 Cobra coupe
blue $35

1831-1 64 Chaparral 2
white $35

1832-1 65 Comet Exterminator
red $35

1833-1 65 Ford Lola T-70, 35
blue $35

K&B 1/32 CLEAR CAR BODIES

Clear bodies were vacuformed from butyrate plastic. They were blistercarded on a "Model Rama Pit Stop" card with a decal sheet and sold for 89 cents. Typical collector's price: $10.

1321 32 Ford coupe (1964–67)
$10

1322 32 Ford two-door sedan (1964–67)
$10

1323 Ferrari GT (1964–67) $10

1324 Porsche RSK (1964–67) $10

1325 Porsche GT (1964–67) $10

1326 Lister Corvette (1964–67)
$7

1327 Jaguar XKE (1964–67) $10

1328 Corvette Sting Ray (1964–67)
$10

1329 BRM (1964–67) $10

1330 Indy Car (1964–67) $10

1331 Southern California Sportsman (1964–65)
$10

1332 Cooper F-1 (1964–67) $10

K&B 1/25 SCALE CAR KITS

308 Dragmaster 64 $100
Aluminum frame and wheels, spring-loaded pick up arm, "German Slick" tires, decals. More a frame than a car, though it does have a driver's head. No motor—drag enthusiasts would buy or make their own. Originally $6.95.

The 1800 and 1801 kits were K&B's first large scale kits and the only ones issued in 1/25 scale. Clear windows molded into the injection-molded body. Decals. Challenger aluminum chassis and wheels with chrome plastic spoked-wheel inserts. Tires stamped "Goodyear." Challenger motor. Originally sold for $8.

1800 64 Ford GT coupe (1965), 36

white $125

A GT-40 LeMans racer. Body based on the prototype. Also issued by Aurora as a model kit. Wheels attach to threaded axle. $7. Reissued as 1811.

1801 Shelby Cobra Daytona GT (1965), 36

medium blue-gray $130

Model Car & Track (April 1965) criticized the shape of windows and headlights but praised the car's performance. Wheels attach to threaded axle. $7. Reissued as 1812. The Japanese company Otaki copied his car, making a few changes in details and molding it in red-orange plastic.

K&B 1/24 CHALLENGER CAR KITS

These kits followed the 1/25 kits but contained new features: Posi-Lok wheel attachments, and most received improved 6-volt Super Challenger motors.

1802 65 Porsche 906/916 (1965), 36

silver gray $125

Porsche supplied K&B with design data. Issued with Challenger motor before Super Challenger was available. Box art by Jack Leynnwood. $7. Reissued as 1813.

1803 Ferrari 250 GTO/64 (1965), 36

maroon $125

Model Car & Track (June 1966) notes model is based on Ferrari belonging to English sports car buff George Drummond, down to tag number "M09-1553." Issued with Challenger motor before Super Challenger was available. $7. Reissued as 1814.

1804 65 Sebring Chaparral (1966–67), 36

white $130

Super Challenger motor. Posi-Lok wheels. $8.

1805 65 Lola T-70 (1966–67), 36

metallic blue $130

Miniature Auto (May 1966) praised the body as a "real work of art," but noted it wasn't accurate. Also noted decals don't match the real car, especially the "Firestone" decal for a car which ran on Goodyear tires. Super Challenger motor. Posi-Lok wheels. $8.

1806 330 P2 Ferrari (1966–67), 36

metallic maroon $150

Super Challenger motor. Posi-Lok wheels. $8.

1811 Ford GT (1966–67)

white $150

Reissue of 1800 in a new white box showing car's profile. Motor upgraded to Super Challenger and wheels attach with Posi-Lok. $8.

1812 Ford Cobra coupe (1966–67)

light metallic blue $175

Reissue of 1801 in a new white box with new art showing only the profile of the car. Lighter metalflake blue replaces earlier blue plastic. Old box art is on box insert. Body mold retooled to add glue-on rear spoiler, rivets and two air scoops on the hood, and brake vents on the sides; changes reflect modifications made by Ford to the original Cobra prototype and incorporated into the car that raced LeMans in 1964 and 1965. Motor upgraded to Super Challenger and wheels attach with Posi-Lok. $7.95.

1813 Porsche 906/916 (1966–67)

silvery gray $150

Reissue of 1802 in a new white box showing car's profile. *Old box art is on box insert. Motor upgraded to Super Challenger. Posi-Lok wheels. $7.95.*

1814 Ferrari 250 GTO/64 (1966–67)

maroon $150

Reissue of 1803 in a new white box showing car's profile. *Old box art is on box insert. Motor upgraded to Super Challenger. Posi-Lok wheels. $7.95.*

K&B 1/24 READY TO RUN CARS

1850 64 Ford Lotus 30 Charger (1965–67)

orange $100

green $100

Plastic body shell; no metal chassis. Royal Bobcat motor mounted as sidewinder. Posi-Lok wheels. Jose Rodriguez, Jr., of Car Model noted body detailing was poor and attributed it to cost cutting. $9.95. Rugged construction made this a popular rental car at commercial slot raceways.

1851 Cooper F-1 Wildcat (1966–67)

white $115

Plastic body shell; no metal chassis. Wildcat 9-volt motor. Posi-Lok wheels. $8.95.

1852 The Sportsman (1966–67)

dark red $150

Clear vacuformed body painted inside. One-piece aluminum chassis, fall away pickup. Royal Bobcat motor *mounted as sidewinder. Posi-Lok wheels. Model of a quarter-mile super-modified stocker. $10.95.*

1853 65 Mako Shark (1966–67)
blue metalflake body $150
Vacuformed body. Kangaroo chassis. Hellcat motor mounted as sidewinder. Cortina Brake. $13.95 Superkit.

1854 McLaren Mark 2 (1966–67)
white $150
Vacuformed body. Nonadjustable metal chassis, Super Challenger motor. "K&B" decal. Based on no. 97 car of Charlie Hayes, sponsored by K&B. $6.95.

1876 Chaparral 2D (1967)
white $150
Vacuformed body. Kangaroo chassis. Jaguar motor. Hells Bells sponge tires. $10.95.

1876 Alfa Romeo Canguro
Announced in 1967, but never issued. Planned features: injection-molded body, Hellcat motor mounted as sidewinder, priced $8. With Cortina brake as Superkit, $13.95.

1877 65 Ford GTX-1 roadster
Announced in 1967, but never issued. Planned features: injection-molded body, Hellcat motor mounted as sidewinder, priced at $8. With Cortina brake as Superkit, $13.95.

1878 Batmobile (1966), 39
black $600
Vacuformed body, injection-molded windshield, chrome-plated parts, red body stripes, Hellcat motor mounted as sidewinder, Cortina brake, blinking red Batlight, $14.95. K&B made this car after Aurora 1/32 static model became a runaway bestseller. K&B President John Brodbeck noted the slot car "laid an egg" because it was a poor racer. K&B had a license for the Green Hornet's Black Beauty, but never issued the car.

1879 Ford-Cobra Bordinat
Announced in 1967, but never issued. Planned features: injection-molded body, Hellcat motor, Cortina brake, $13.95.

1895 Blue Monster (1966–67)
$500
Vacuformed body painted metallic blue, yellow stripes. McLaren I car body. One-piece aluminum chassis. K&B ran a 1966 "Blue Monster Bonanza" contest in race centers to publicize introduction of the new Blue Monster motor. Advertised as super-fast, reviewers in slot magazines rated it good, not outstanding. $12.95.

Jupiter
Announced in 1967, but never issued. $13.95

Ford GT Mark II (1967)
blue, fogged silver paint $200
Hot Shot Inline chassis. Inline 26-D Jaguar motor. Cortina brake. $12. Final K&B slot car.

K&B INJECTION-MOLDED 1/25 AND 1/24 BODIES

Kits had the same injection-molded bodies as in the motorized kits above, with clear and chrome parts and decal sheet. $1.29.

1800-1 Ford GT coupe 1/25
white $30

1801-1 Ford Cobra coupe 1/25
Medium blue-gray $30

1802-1 Porsche 906/916
silver gray $30

1803-1 Ferrari GTO/LM
maroon $30

1804-1 Chaparral 2
white $40

1805-1 Ford Lola T-70
blue $40

1806-1 Ferrari 330 P2
metallic maroon $50

1850-1 Lotus 30
orange $25
green $25

K&B 1/25 SCALE CLEAR BODIES

Bodies were vacuformed from clear butyrate plastic. Sold for 98 cents. Today collectors pay around $10.

1301 Corvette Sting Ray
split window $10

1302 Jaguar XKE $10

1303 32 Ford coupe $10

1304 59 Corvette hardtop $10

1305 32 Ford Victoria $10

1306 Maserati Tipo 61 Birdcage sport coupe
$10

MOTORS

Although hard to find, all the motors listed below can be purchased in the $10–$25 range.

1500 K&B Royal Bobcat 36D Mabuchi
$10–$25
9-volt, yellow can, white endbell

1501 K&B Bobcat 36D Mabuchi
$10–$25
12-volt, yellow can, white endbell

1502 K&B Challenger Aurora-built sidewinder
$10–$25
12-volt, bare metal and black or white plastic

1503/1504 K&B Super Challenger Aurora-built sidewinder
$10–$25
6-volt, bare metal and black plastic. Major visible difference between a Super Challenger and Challenger is the cylinder containing the commutator—added to the side of the Super Challenger.

1505 K&B Wildcat 16D Mabuchi
$10–$25
9-volt, yellow can, white endbell

1506 K&B Cougar 13D Mabuchi
$10–$25
9-volt, yellow can, white endbell

1508 K&B Jaguar 26D Mabuchi
$10–$25
3-volt, chrome can, white endbell

K&B Blue Monster 36D Aurora-built
$10–$25
6-volt, black endplates, motor held together with blue metal clips. The version of the Hellcat (1510) used in the K&B Blue Monster (1895) and not sold separately.

1510 K&B Hellcat 36D Aurora-built
$10–$25
12-volt, black endplates, motor held together with black metal clips. K&B version of Aurora Blue Monster.

1553 K&B Challenger Aurora-built sidewinder
$10–$25
12-volt, bare metal and black or white plastic. Stock motor of early K&B kits; same as the K&B 1502 and Aurora 3250 A-Jet.

3250 Aurora A-Jet Aurora-built sidewinder
$10–$25
12-volt, bare metal and black or white plastic. Stock motor of early Aurora A-Jet cars; same as the K&B Challenger 1502 and 1553.